Rubber Manufacturing Company

Manufacturers of mechanical rubber goods of every kind

Rubber Manufacturing Company

Manufacturers of mechanical rubber goods of every kind

ISBN/EAN: 9783337226794

Printed in Europe, USA, Canada, Australia, Japan

Cover: Foto ©Andreas Hilbeck / pixelio.de

More available books at **www.hansebooks.com**

THE GUTTA PERCHA & RUBBER MFG CO.
OF TORONTO LTD
RUBBER GOODS

OFFICES AND WAREROOMS:

61 & 63 FRONT ST. WEST,
TORONTO.

PRICE LIST,—EDITION 1896-7

Superseding all Previous Issues.

HE GUTTA PERCHA
& RUBBER MFG. CO.

OF TORONTO, Ltd.

MANUFACTURERS OF

MECHANICAL RUBBER GOODS

OF EVERY KIND,

RUBBER BELTING,

PACKINGS, HOSE,

Fire Dept. Supplies,

ALSO

Mackintoshes and Rubber Clothing.

HEAD OFFICE AND WAREROOMS:

61-63 FRONT STREET WEST,

TORONTO, ONT.

☞ For General Index see pages 103 to 108.

TO THE TRADE

DEALERS wishing quotations will oblige us by specifying the goods wanted, and we will promptly furnish quotations as desired.

The variety of Rubber Goods which we manufacture, and the different Trades using them are so diversified, that we have found this method of furnishing discounts to meet special wants more satisfactorily than issuing a complete discount sheet comprising all our manufactures.

Our Factories are the only Rubber Factories in Toronto.

They are situated in West Lodge and O'Hara Avenues, Parkdale, and are equipped with the latest and most improved machinery known.

We manufacture Belting, Packing, Hose, Moulded Goods, Carriage Cloths, Drills, Mackintosh Clothing, Rubber Clothing, Tubing and all kinds of Rubber Goods for Mechanical purposes.

We employ none but Skilled and Experienced Workmen.

Should you require any Rubber Goods not mentioned in this list kindly write to us and we will cheerfully furnish prices and full information.

Yours truly,

THE GUTTA PERCHA & RUBBER MFG. CO.

OF TORONTO (Ltd.)

61 & 63 FRONT STREET WEST,
TORONTO, CANADA.

Useful Information about Rubber Belting.

A S compared with leather, rubber belting is not only much cheaper, but under certain conditions is capable of giving longer and better service. Unlike leather belting, it can be used in all kinds of weather, or in damp places. It is of an even, uniform width and thickness throughout, and on account of its smooth, metallic surface the contact between the pulley and the belting is more perfect, thus obtaining maximum power. It will withstand without injury a considerable amount of heat, and retain its flexibility in the coldest of weather.

CARE AND USE.

In selecting belts for special uses, ALLOW SUFFICIENT WIDTH, so that they will run without slipping and still be moderately slack. Tight belts add greatly to the friction on bearings, and waste much power. From 25 to 40 per cent. of the power used in most mills is required to drive the shafting alone. Tight belts are responsible for much of this waste.

Where belts run at an angle of 45 degrees or less, apply power when possible, so that the under side of the belt will do the driving. This allows the upper side to sag, increasing the arc of pulley contact, and, consequently, the driving power.

Use pulleys as large as consistent, in order that the stretch on the outside and compression on the inside, caused by bending the belt around pulleys, may be reduced as much as possible. The thicker the belt, the larger the pulley should be on which it is used.

Shafting should be hung perfectly level, and parallel, with pulleys in line, and no projecting timber or flooring should come in contact with the belting. Experience has shown that neglect of one or the other of these essentials causes a very large part of all damage to belting.

NEVER ALLOW animal or mineral oils or grease to come in contact with rubber belting; they are injurious to it.

Should the surface of the belt be peeled or rubbed by slipping, the following mixture may be applied with a brush, and will produce a fine surface. Let it dry before running the belt :

Useful Information about Rubber Belting
(Continued).

FORMULA.—Equal parts of red lead, black lead, French yellow and litharge. Mix with boiled linseed oil, and add enough Japan to make it dry quickly.

When from accumulation of dust or other similar causes, a rubber belt slips, it may be moistened LIGHTLY on the inner side with BOILED LINSEED OIL applied with a brush.

When a tightening pulley is used it should be applied to the slack side of the belt, near the smaller pulley.

As the adhesion of the belt to the pulley surface is a vital element in all calculations of power transmission, it is important to note that the adhesion of rubber belting to the various forms of pulley surface is from 40 to 80 per cent. greater than that of leather belting, therefore, rubber belting must transmit more power than leather.

DO NOT OVERTAX BELTS nor run them tighter than necessary. In other words, DON'T SEND A BOY TO DO A MAN'S WORK!

A four ply rubber belt is equal to a single leather belt. A six ply rubber be t is equal to a double leather belt.

LACING OF BELTS.

This deserves careful attention. Ignorance or carelessness in lacing leads to frequent annoyance and frequent damage or destruction of the belt. THE ENDS OF THE BELT SHOULD BE PERFECTLY SQUARED. Lace holes should be cut with a sharp oval or round punch. In lacing narrow belts, butt the two ends together, making two rows of hol s in each. (thus obtaining a double hold) being particular that the holes in the second row are not punched immediately behind holes in the front row, but midway between them as shown in sketch.

For wide belts, in addition, put a thin piece of leather or rubber on the back to strengthen the joint, equal in length to the width of the belt, and sew or rivet it to the belt, as shown in cuts of back splice on p. 6

Lacing of belts can be done best by the aid of belt clamps secured firmly to each end of the belt, and drawn together by bolts running parallel with and outside the edges of the belt.

RULE FOR MEASURING BELTING IN ROLLS WHEN CLOSELY COILED.

RULE.—The sum of the diameter of the roll taken in inches and the diameter of the centre hole in inches, multiplied by the number of coils in the roll, and the product multiplied by the decimal .1319, equals very closely the number of feet of belting in the roll.

BELTING DON'TS.

Don't forget that there is nothing like rubber if properly used.

Don't order your belt too narrow or too light.

Don't cut the lace holes ragged or too large.

Don't cut lace holes too near the ends of the belt.

Don't cut or lace the belt crooked ; use a square.

Don't cut one lace hole behind another when cutting two rows.

Don't condemn a belt that breaks because of improper lacing.

Don't expect good wear from belts run on bad pulleys.

Don't use a pulley narrower than the width of the belt.

Don't cut belt too short, or it may tear out at lace holes or break.

Don't allow the edges or face of belts to run against any obstruction.

Don't forget that rubber belts will stand greater heat than any other kind.

Don't forget that rubber belting will transmit more power than any other kind.

Don't forget that grease and oil are injurious to rubber belts and will destroy them.

Don't forget that cheap belts are made on light duck ; better grades on heavy duck.

Don't forget that the strength of a belt depends upon the number of plies and weight of duck in it.

Don't forget that the cost of rubber belting is much below that of good leather.

Don't forget that rubber belts will run in damp or wet places (but not in water) where other belts fail.

Don't run the seam side of the belt to the pulley unless pulley is crowned $\frac{1}{8}$ inch per ft. or more.

Don't allow a belt to run with an air blister in it ; cut out the blistered portion AT ONCE and thus save the rest of the belt.

Don't use a rough plank when shifting belts : shippers with rollers that press upon the face of the belt, instead of on the edge, should be used.

Methods of Fastening Rubber Belts.

BACK SPLICE

SIDE VIEW OF BACK SPLICE

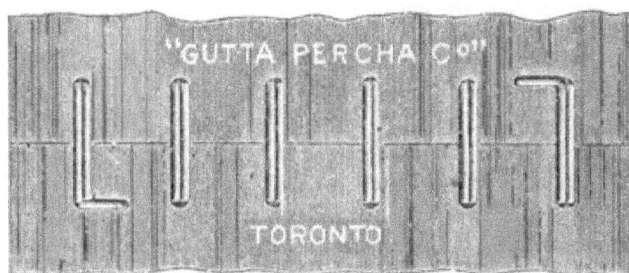

WIRE LACING—PULLEY SIDE.

WIRE LACING—OUTSIDE.

THIS wire lacing is made from a composition which makes it practically adapted for the purpose for which it is intended, and is in many cases an excellent substitute for lace leather or other belt fastenings.

Tighteners may be run on belts so laced, and this method of fastening is a good substitute for endless belts, especially for short or narrow belts, and at less cost.

Methods of Fastening Rubber Belts—*(Continued).*

LACING.

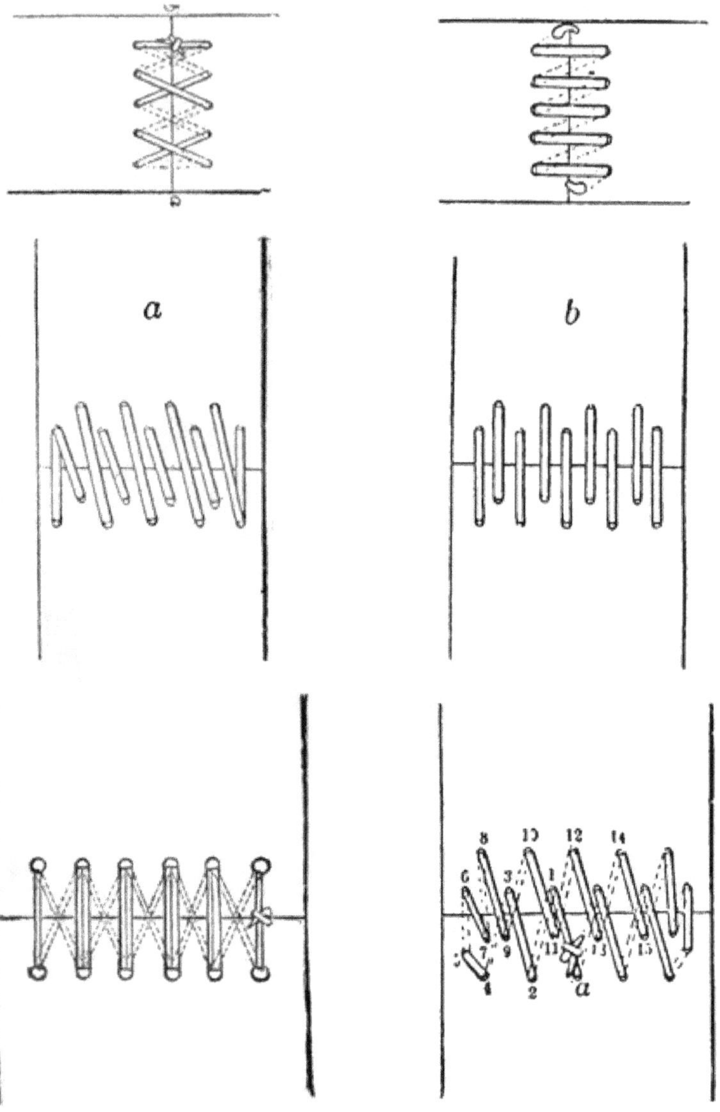

Methods of Fastening Rubber Belts—*(Continued).*

HOOKS AND STUDS.

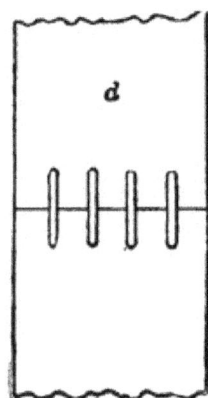

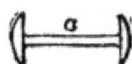

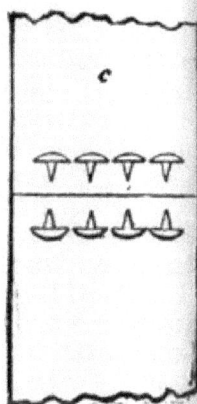

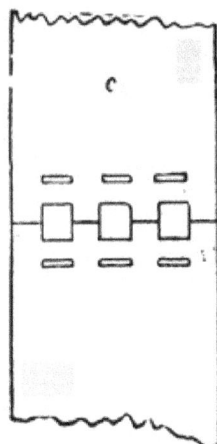

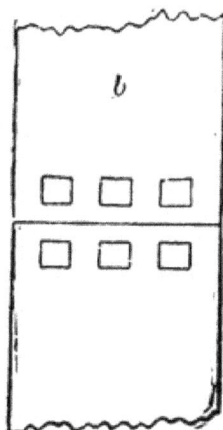

ELEVATOR BELTING.

We make a specialty of Elevator Belting and have filled the largest contracts awarded in this country.

Below is a partial list of Elevators we have supplied.

Canadian Pacific Railway Co. Elevators, Fort William and North Bay.
Grand Trunk Railway.
Ogilvie Milling Co.—17 Elevators.
Northern Elevator Co.—6 Elevators.
Lake of Woods Milling Co., Keewatin, and branches.
Carnduff Mill & Elevator Co.—2 Elevators.
Martin Elevator Co.———Smith & Brigham.
Canadian Alliance Farming Co.
Roblin & Armitage—3 Elevators.
Mann & Durham.
R. D. Martin—3 Elevators.
Morden Farmers Elevator Co.
Moosomin Elevator Co.
Rapid City Elevator Co.
Southern Manitoba Elevator Co.
Treherne Farmers Elevator Co.
E. A. Baker & Co.
Ceater Farmers Elevator Co.
Alexander Farmers Elevator Co.
Burnside Farmers Elevator Co.
Carson & Carson.——— H. S. Patterson.
Parish & Lindsay.———T. E. M. Banting.
Bateman & Chapin.
Carman Farmers Elevator Co.
E. Simpson.———J. S. Brisco.
Glenboro Farmers Elevator Co.
M. J. Umac & Co.
Holland Farmers Elevator Co.
Patrons Elevator Co.——Belgonia Elevator Co.
Ironside, Notherall & Co.
D. H. McMillan & Bro.
Donald & Frazer.———Grenfel Elevator Co.
R. L. Campbell.———E. O. Rilley.
E. A. Holmes & Co.———D. H. McMillan & Co.
Ironsides & Kerr.———John Schwartz.

For List Prices see Pages 16 and 17.

STITCHED BELTING.

WE MAKE TWO QUALITIES.

"MALTESE CROSS" and "BEAVER" BRANDS.

For Descriptions see next page.

MADE to order on short notice—not carried in stock.

In the manufacture of this belting the plies of rubber coated duck are thoroughly united and **stretched**, and before putting on the outside, or cover, the plies are **stitched together with strong cord,** the rows of stitching being about one inch apart and running the entire length of the belt, and so put in that should the loops of the stitches wear off the cord remains in the belt **acting like rivets** to hold the plies firmly together. The outside rubber, or cover, is then put on **seamless** so that it cannot open, and the belt is again stretched and vulcanized, making a solid and compact body.

We also manufacture **Endless Belts stitched** in the same way.

For List Prices see Pages 16 and 17.

STITCHED BELTING

(Continued),

"MALTESE CROSS" Brand.—"The best that can be produced" is our aim with respect to any goods bearing our "Maltese Cross" brand or trade mark. The heaviest duck and the best materials throughout that are known to the trade are employed in making this belt. The rubber "friction" holding the plies of duck together possesses the greatest possible strength and tenacity, in addition to which the plies are sewn firmly together with rows of heavy cord as described on preceding page. The cover is put on seamless and is of a specially fine quality, compounded to produce the best finish and most durable wearing surface.

Those wishing to obtain the highest grade belting in the market, and who are willing to pay the necessary extra cost, will find this brand the best possible equivalent for the money.

N. B.—Customers wishing this belt will kindly not fail to specify on each order that they wish the "Maltese Cross" brand ; as, owing to its extra price and the fact of its having to be made specially in every instance, this brand would not regularly be sent except when clearly specified by name in the order.

"BEAVER" Brand.—This will be known as the "Gutta Percha Co's." regular grade of Stitched Belting. It is made up in the same general manner as our "Maltese Cross" brand, and is intended to be equal or superior to any stitched belting other than the "Maltese Cross." It is made on heavy duck, and all the materials used in it are of fine quality such as are used only in high grade belting.

List prices same as for regular rubber belting.
See Pages 16 and 17.

"MONARCH BRAND"

Superior Rubber Belting.

TRADE   MARK.

A SPECIALLY fine quality, suitable for hard service and superior to the finest belting that used to be sold "years ago."

Strong and durable for heavy work where low priced belting fails.

The "Monarch" brand of Belting is made on **extra heavy Cotton Duck** woven specially for the purpose. **The friction** is made of **carefully selected Rubber** of the kinds **best adapted for holding the plies firmly together, the finish is smooth**, giving the Belt a fine appearance. **It is stretched** to the utmost limit of safety in the process of manufacture, by **improved Machinery used only in our Factories**, and is **Vulcanized and pressed under Tension** in our heavy hydraulic presses. By this process **we vulcanize most of the stretch out of the Belts. We fully guarantee it**, but the **excellence of its quality**, which we are **determined to maintain**, prohibits our entering any competition as to price on this brand.

For List Prices see Pages 16 and 17.

" RED STRIP " BRAND
Extra Heavy Rubber Belting.

OUR Patent **"Red Strip"** Rubber Belting is made on **extra heavy duck** woven specially for this Company, and has a **red strip of pure rubber running the entire length of the belt,** directly under the lap, which **prevents any tendency to split at the seam,** and strengthens the belt. Our **"Red Strip"** belt is also stretched upon our **patent hydraulic stretcher** which is the most perfect and effective machine of its kind in the world. In consequence it will retain a perfect uniformity of width and thickness, and will remain unaffected by heat or cold. **This brand is generally sold by dealers as the "best belting."**

Carried in stock in all usual sizes. Other sizes made to order on short notice.

For List Prices see Pages 16 and 17.

"LION" BELTING.

IN order to meet the market for a lower priced belt than the cost of our other brands will warrant, we have given this the distinctive name of **"Lion."** It corresponds with or is superior to the so-called **"Standard," "Extra,"** and **"Extra Standard"** goods. We do not offer it as the best we manufacture; but believe it to be the best belt for the money in the market. The demand for it has steadily increased, because found so generally reliable and satisfactory.

Carried in stock in all usual sizes. Other sizes made to order on short notice.

For List Prices see Pages 16 and 17.

"THRESHER" BELTS.

For List Prices see page 16.

When made endless, 3 feet extra charged for Splice.

These we make regularly in three grades, namely :

"Monarch" brand, a special quality.

"Red Strip" brand, a heavy, superior grade.

"Lion" brand, extra quality ; the popular grade.

While the above brands correspond in name with the three grades of belting we make regularly for general use, we have learned from long experience in manufacturing belting for the agricultural trade, that for Threshers' use the Drive Belts should be constructed in a special manner to meet the peculiar requirements of that service.

All of our Thresher Belts are therefore made specially with the view of obtaining the best possible results in such service. No usage is more severe than that to which Thresher Drive Belts are subjected. Purchasers will do well to bear this in mind and select the best grades when ordering.

N.B.—Should an air blister appear in the belt, cut out the blistered portion IMMEDIATELY and lace the belt. If allowed to run the air will be forced between the plies of duck throughout the entire length and the whole belt will thus be ruined ; whereas, if the blistered portion is cut out immediately the balance of the belt may be saved.

Price List for All Grades

OF

RUBBER BELTING.

These List Prices apply to our **"Monarch," "Red Strip" and "Lion" Grades,** as well as to our **"Elevator Belting," "Stitched Belting" and "Thresher" Belts,** and is the List adopted and universally used throughout the Trade.

Width, in Inches.	2 Ply. Per ft.	3 Ply. Per ft.	4 Ply. Per ft.	5 Ply. Per ft.	6 Ply. Per ft.	7 Ply. Per ft.	8 Ply. Per ft.
1	$ .07	$ .09	$ .11	....	....	....	....
1¼	.09	.11	.13	....	....	....	....
1½	.11	.13	.15	$ .19	....	....	....
1¾	.13	.15	.17	.21	....	....	....
2	.15	.17	.21	.26	$ .31	....	....
2½	.18	.22	.26	.33	.39	....	....
3	.22	.26	.31	.39	.47	....	....
3½	.26	.30	.37	.46	.56	....	....
4	.30	.34	.42	.53	.63	....	..
4½	.33	.39	.47	.59	.71	....	....
5	.36	.43	.52	.65	.78	....	....
6	.43	.52	.62	.78	.93	$1.08	$1.24
7	.51	.60	.73	.91	1.10	1.28	1.46
8	.59	.70	.84	1.05	1.26	1.47	1.68
9	.67	.80	.95	1.18	1.42	1.66	1.90
10	.75	.90	1.07	1.33	1.60	1.87	2.14
11	.83	1.00	1.18	1.47	1.77	2.06	2.36
12	.91	1.08	1.30	1.62	1.95	2.27	2.60
13	1.00	1.18	1.42	1.77	2.13	2.48	2.84
14	1.08	1.28	1.54	1.92	2.31	2.69	3.08
15	1.16	1.38	1.66	2.07	2.49	2.90	3.32

Continued on Next Page.

Patent Stretched Rubber Belting.

(Continued).

Width, in Inches.	2 Ply. Per ft.	3 Ply Per ft.	4 Ply Per ft.	5 Ply Per ft.	6 Ply Per ft.	7 Ply Per ft.	8 Ply Per ft.
16	$1.25	$1.50	$1.78	$2.22	$ 2.67	$ 3.11	$ 3.56
18	1.41	1.70	2.02	2.52	3.03	3.53	4.04
20	1.58	1.90	2.26	2.82	3.39	3.95	4.52
22	1.76	2.12	2.52	3.15	3.78	4.41	5.04
24	1.96	2.36	2.80	3.50	4.20	4.90	5.60
26	2.18	2.60	3.08	3.85	4.62	5.39	6.16
28	2.42	2.84	3.36	4.20	5.04	5.88	6.72
30	....	....	3.64	4.55	5.46	6.37	7.28
32	....	....	3.92	4.90	5.88	6.86	7.84
34	....	....	4.20	5.25	6.30	7.35	8.40
36	....	....	4.48	5.60	6.72	7.84	8.96
38	....	....	4.76	5.95	7.14	8.33	9.52
40	....	....	5.04	6.30	7.56	8.82	10.08
42	....	....	5.32	6.65	7.98	9.31	10.64
44	....	...	5.60	7.00	8.40	9.80	11.20
46	....	....	5.88	7.35	8.82	10.29	11.76
48	....	....	6.16	7.70	9.24	10.78	12.32
50	....	....	6.44	8.05	9.66	11.27	12.88
52	....	....	....	8.40	10.08	11.76	13.44
54	....	....	....	8.75	10.50	12.25	14.00
56	....	....	....	9.10	10.92	12.74	14.56
58	....	....	....	9.45	11.34	13.23	15.12
60	....	....	....	9.80	11.76	13.72	15.68

ANY WIDTH UP TO SEVENTY-TWO INCHES.

Intermediate widths at proportionate prices. **Regular or full rolls contain 350 to 400 feet,** but we cut or make to order any width or length required.

Endless Belts made to order, on which there will be three extra feet charged for the splice. We do not advise endless belts in narrow widths or short lengths.

☞ **The above list prices apply to all grades of Rubber Belting, the discounts from these list prices varying according to quality.**

EMERY AND SAND BELTS.

NOT CARRIED IN STOCK, BUT MADE
TO ORDER ON SHORT NOTICE.

THESE Belts are made endless to any lengths ordered, and in any number of plies to suit customers.

The Duck used in their construction is specially adapted to the purpose. The plies are held firmly together by a fine quality of rubber, and the outer surface has the Duck exposed ready for the coating of emery or sand.

PRICE LIST :

Width, in Inches.	2 ply per ft.	3 ply per ft.	4 ply per ft.	5 ply per ft.	6 ply per ft.	7 ply per ft.	8 ply per ft.
1	$ .07	$ .09	$ .11	....	....	....	....
1¼	.09	.11	.13	....	....	...	....
1½	.11	.13	.15	$ .19	....	...	....
1¾	.13	.15	.17	.21	....	....	...
2	.15	.17	.21	.26	$ .31	....	....
2½	.18	.22	.26	.33	.39	....	....
3	.22	.26	.31	.39	.47	....	...
3½	.26	.30	.37	.46	.56	....	....
4	.30	.34	.42	.53	.63	...	....
4½	.33	.39	.47	.59	.71	....	....
5	.36	.43	.52	.65	.78	....	...
6	.43	.52	.62	.78	.93	$1.08	$1.24
7	.51	.60	.73	.91	1.10	1.28	1.46
8	.59	.70	.84	1.05	1.26	1.47	1.68
9	.67	.80	.95	1.18	1.42	1.66	1.90
10	.75	.90	1.07	1.33	1.60	1.87	2.14
11	.83	1.00	1.18	1.47	1.77	2.06	2.36
12	.91	1.08	1.30	1.62	1.95	2.27	2.60
13	1.00	1.18	1.42	1.77	2.13	2.48	2.84
14	1.08	1.28	1.54	1.92	2.31	2.69	3.08
15	1.16	1.38	1.66	2.07	2.49	2.90	3.32

N.B.—In ordering state length, width and number of plies desired.

PLUMBAGO SHEET PACKING.

Self-Vulcanizing.

WILL vulcanize when in place and make a perfect joint. Specially adapted for use on uneven surfaces. Two or more thicknesses can be put together, and under heat or pressure become as one piece. Kept in stock in sheets $\frac{1}{16}$ and $\frac{1}{8}$ of an inch thick, other sizes made to order on short notice.

LIST PRICES.

Pure, Plain,   -   -   -   per lb. 70c.
"   with Wire Insertion,   -   "   80c.
"   " Duck   "   -   "   90c.

DIRECTIONS FOR USING PLUMBAGO PACKING.

Place the packing in position and screw up the nuts tight **while cold**; let the steam on enough to warm the packing, which, being unvulcanized, will soften when steam is first applied to it. Follow up the joint carefully until there is no escape of steam, and the pack-ing has become hard and fitted to the joint. Cut bolt holes a little less in diameter than the size of bolts. Cut the inside hole $\frac{1}{8}$ inch larger all round.

STEAM SHEET PACKING.

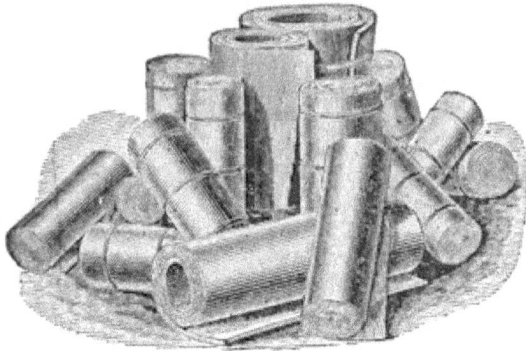

Made in several qualities, and all in three ways, viz :

"PLAIN"=Rubber Outside with Cloth Insertion.
"C.O.S."=Cloth on One Side.
"C.B.S."=Cloth on Both Sides.

THICKNESS.	1 PLY.	2 PLY.	3 PLY.	4 PLY.
1-64 inch	70 cts.	......	......	......
1-32 "	65 "	......	......	......
1-16 "	60 "	63 cts.	66 cts.	......
3-32 "	55 "	58 "	61 "	......
1-8 "	55 "	55 "	58 "	61 cts.
5-32 "	55 "	55 "	58 "	61 "
3-16 "	55 "	55 "	55 "	58 "
1-4 "	55 "	55 "	55 "	55 "

One ply of Cloth to every $\frac{1}{16}$ inch thickness.

Three Cents per pound **additional** will be charged for **each extra ply of cloth. Each cloth, whether insertion or on outside, to count as One Ply.**

All Cloth Insertion or Plain Packing is about one yard wide, and any length desired.

Wire Insertion Packing,

PLAIN RUBBER.

Price per lb. $\frac{1}{16}$ in. thick and upwards, - $0.80

Pure Rubber Sheet Packing.

WITHOUT CLOTH.

List Price,   -   -   - $1.40 per lb.

MADE regularly in rolls about 36 inches in width, of any thickness or length desired, and in a variety of qualities to suit purpose for which it is intended.

Special widths, not exceeding 72 inches, or long strips of almost any dimensions, in rectangular shape, may be made on orders for suitable quantities and at special prices.

N.B.– In ordering strips please state the SHORTEST lengths in which they can be taken. Also please note that triangular or irregular shaped strips cannot be made without suitable iron moulds which must be provided by the purchaser.

We append a list of some of the Pure Sheet Packing Stocks we supply, together with the net selling price per pound of each. These prices apply only to the Packings when supplied in regular stock width, and cut straight across the piece.

P.G. Sheet,	" A " quality	.........per lb.,	50c. net
"	"	" B "	"	"	60c. "
"	"	" C "	"	....	"	70c. "
"	"	" D "	"	"	80c. "
"	"	" E "	"	....	"	90c. "
"	"	" 620 "	"	soft....	"	$1.50 "

For cutting rubber use a sharp knife and keep it wet.

PISTON PACKINGS.

"TUCK'S ROUND."   **"SQUARE DUCK."**

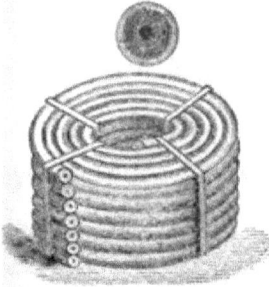 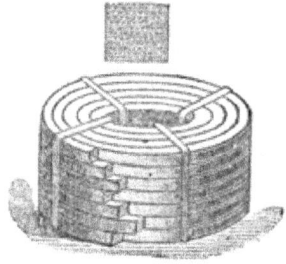

List Price,   - - -   per lb. 85 cts.

Made regularly in lengths of 12 feet each, and in izes from ¼ to 2 inches diameter.

SQUARE PISTON PACKING.

"RUBBER BACK."

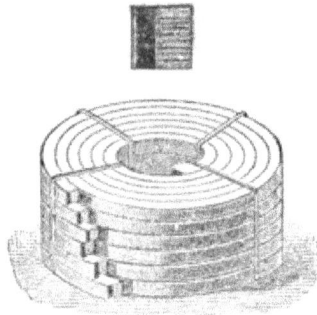

List Price,   - - - -   per lb. $1.00

Usual sizes in stock.

PISTON PACKINGS.—*(Continued)*.

SPECIAL "HYDRAULIC" OR "ELEVATOR" PACKING.

Made of fine Duck and white Rubber, very firm, just the thing for packing hydraulic elevators. Made on short notice in any lengths up to 20 feet, on orders for 50 lbs. or upwards of one size. Usual length of coils 12 ft. each.

List Price.................. ....per lb. $1.25

"VICTORIA" ROUND PACKING.

SELF-VULCANIZING.

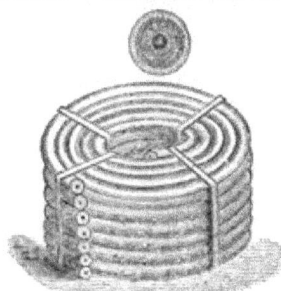

Made with a round core of self-vulcanizing compound, similar to our Plumbago Packing, and of loose woven Duck so as to be very flexible when applied to the Piston Rod. This packing is also partially self lubricating, so as not to score the rods.

List Price........................per lb. $1.00

Made to order on short notice in 12 foot lengths and in any size up to two inches diameter.

"GUTTAPERCH"
BRAND.

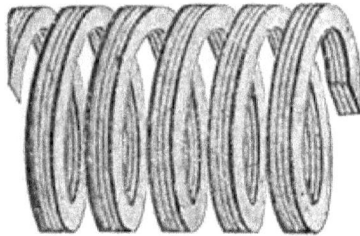

SPIRAL PISTON PACKING.
ANTI-FRICTION.
SELF-LUBRICATING.

MADE either with Rubber Cushion in the centre, or with Rubber on both outside surfaces and Duck in the centre, as shown in cut. By our improved lubricating treatment we eliminate the objectionable features noticed in similar packings introduced by other makers. A valuable feature of this packing is that both dealers and consumers can profitably carry it in stock, as it is always ready for instant use, and there is little or no waste.

We can fill orders promptly from stock for the following sizes :—3/16, 1/4, 5/16, 3/8, 7/16. 1/2, 9/16, 5/8. 11/16, 3/4, 13/16, 7/8, 14/16 and 1 inch, and make other larger sizes up to 2 inches, to order on short notice.

Each size is neatly packed in a telescope box containing a coil of about 12 ft. The sizes are plainly marked in attractive labels, and full directions accompany each box. This is one of the most economical and best Piston Packings made, and if properly used will give universal satisfaction.

List Price Per Pound, $1.20.

☞**Don't screw the glands up too tight as his Packing is intended to expand in the Box.**

"Elastic Ring" Packing.

"GUTTAPERCH" BRAND.

Rubber Elastic Cushion in Centre or on outsides. We make both

THESE Rings are made to fit perfectly around the Piston Rod, and fill the Stuffing Box. They are subjected to the same lubricating process as our Spiral Packing, by an entirely new method known only to ourselves. These Rings are made to order to any desired size, and orders for them are promptly filled When shipped they are packed in suitable boxes, made specially for the purpose, to keep them free from dirt and grit in transit.

HOW TO ORDER.

Give exact diameter of Piston, Valve or Cut-off Rod to be packed. also the diameter and depth of the Stuffing Box. State number of Rings wanted, and whether "Elastic" or "Sectional Rings" are preferred. When no preference is expressed, we frequently send part Elastic and part Sectional Rings.

N.B.—A few extra Rings or Coils of "Guttaperch Spiral Packing" should always be kept on hand in case of emergency ; it costs no more in the end, and may save many dollars.

Full directions for use accompany each Shipment.

List Price, $1.20 Per Pound.

☞**Don't screw the glands up too tight as this packing is intended to expand in the Box**

"Sectional Ring" Packing.

"GUTTAPERCH" BRAND.

lastic Rubber Cushion either in Centre or outside. We make
both. This cut shows Cushions outside.

THESE are made similar to the "Elastic Rings," with
the exception that they are cut diagonally into
two sections, as shown in cut, so as to perfectly
reak the joint, and provide compensation for wear by
imply tightening the nuts gently, (thus causing the
ings to increase in outside diameter), or adding a new
ing from time to time as needed.

For high-speed Engines, Steam Hammers, Ammonia
'umps, and Engines, where the Piston or Valve rods are
ut of line, this Packing has no equal. Prevents scoring
nd wear on the rod. Is entirely automatic and self-
ubricating, always ready. The lubricating process used
s known only to ourselves.

HOW TO ORDER.

Give exact diameter of Piston, Valve or Cut-off Rod
o be packed, also diameter and depth of Stuffing Box.
State number of rings wanted, and whether "Sectional"
or "Elastic Rings" are preferred. Packed for shipment in suitable boxes, made specially for the purpose,
to keep them free from dirt or grit.

Directions for use accompany each shipment.

List Price, $1.20 Per Pound.

☞ **Don't screw the glands up too tight as
this Packing is intended to expand in the Box.**

PURE SQUARE RUBBER PACKING.

KEPT in stock in all the regular sizes up to 1 inch square and in lengths of about 12 feet each. The quality kept in stock is a fine grade of Rubber of medium softness, suitable for general purposes. Any quality and lengths, other than 12 feet, made specially on orders for sufficient quantity. When a very soft, rich article for packing side lights in vessels or similar purpose is required, our No. 620 stock is admirably suited.

N.B.—In ordering state shortest lengths in which goods can be used.

List Price.......................per lb., $1.50

———

ROUND PURE RUBBER CORD.

Kept in stock in all the regular sizes in a fine quality of medium elasticity, suitable for most all ordinary purposes. Special qualities made to order. Regular stock lengths about 25 feet in each coil ; special lengths made to suit customers.

N.B.—In ordering state shortest lengths in which goods can be used.

List Prices :

Diameter—	1/4	3/8	1/2	5/8	3/4	7/8	1	larger inch.
Price	$2.00	1.75	1.65	1.65	1.60	1.60	1.50	1.50 per lb.

GASKETS AND RINGS.

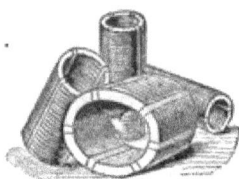

FIBROUS.

/8 inch thick, or less - - per lb., $0.90
/32 " " and upwards - - " 0.80

CLOTH INSERTION.

/16 inch thick, or less - - per lb., $1.25
3/32 " " and upwards - - " 1.00

There is regularly one ply of cloth to every 1/16 inch thickness. Five cents per lb. additional will be charged for each extra ply of cloth.

PURE GUM GASKETS OR RINGS.

Any size and thickness - - per lb., $1.50
Gaskets and Rings cut to order from
    Plumbago Packing (see page 20) - " 1.00

ORDERS FOR SPECIAL SIZES FILLED ON SHORT
NOTICE.

PURE RUBBER VALVES.

MOULDED TO ORDER.

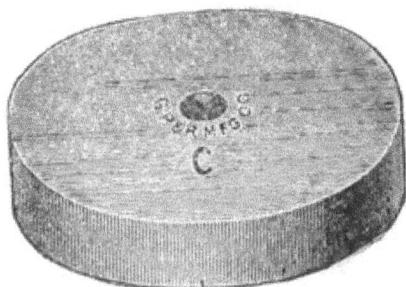

IN order to get the best results from Rubber Valves, the manufacturer should be informed of the conditions under which they are to be used.

We make a specialty in this line, by compounding especially for the varied uses to which valves are put. We do not believe in trying to make one compound answer for all purposes.

Don't expect cheap valves to give the best service. **There is no economy in cheap Rubber Valves.**

When ordering state:

1st—Dimensions.

2nd—Size of hole (if any).

3rd—Thickness.

4th—Round or square, if size admits of any doubt.

5th—For use in hot or cold water.

6th—Soft or medium or hard.

7th—Quote our compound number if possible (see next page).

List Price.................... ....per lb., $1.50.

VALVES—*Continued.*

Compound No. 8.—Gray—Medium in texture, best suited for cold water, but may be used for hot water up to about 185° Fahr. An excellent valve for ordinary pump work at moderate cost.

Compound No. 9.—Gray—A soft valve for hot or cold water. Well adapted to pumps needing soft, flexible valves, foot valves for engines, air pumps, etc.

Compound No. 11.—Red—A soft Antimony marine valve suitable for hot or cold water. One of the finest compounds known for soft valves in danger of oil contact, for condensers and marine work.

Compound No. 440.—Black—Made in three ways, viz: **Medium, Hard or Very Hard.** In ordering state which texture is required. Suitable for hot or cold water pumps and very successfully used where a tough valve is required to withstand heavy pounding. Intended to be used with a straight lift, not to bend.

Compound No. 441.—Gray—The richest, softest and best valve that can be made for cold or hot water where a lively soft valve is wanted.

Compound No. 492.—Red—The finest and softest Antimony valve made for work similar to that for which No. 441 is intended.

Compound No. 605.—Gray—A little softer than No. 8, but not so soft as No. 9. A rich, tough valve for cold or hot water, suitable for straight lift or cup guard.

Compound No. 606.—Gray—Medium, harder than No. 8; not so hard as No. 440 medium. For cold or hot water, very tough, suitable for heavy work and hard pounding where a more flexible valve than No. 440 is required.

List Price for Valves............per lb., $1.50.

NOTE.—All **of above** Valve Compounds **can be supplied upon order in** Sheets **of any width and length.**

List Price for **Valve Sheet**......per lb., $1.40.

4

CAR SPRINGS.

ALL QUALITIES AND SIZES.

Prices, from 35 cts. up to $1.50 per lb.

TRUCK WHEEL TIRES.

Truck Wheels covered with Rubber, any thickness. Vulcanized on the wheels or made to slip on when wheels are flanged.

Prices on Application.

MOULDED GOODS OF ANY SIZE OR PATTERN TO ORDER.

Moulds are required to produce rubber goods in irregular shapes. Parties requiring special moulded articles must provide us with suitable Metal Moulds, (usually iron), for producing them. The cost of such moulds, if provided by us, must be paid by the parties for whom we obtain them. Moulds which are the property of one customer will not be used to make goods for another.

Generally speaking, the greater the mould capacity furnished, the lower will be the cost of producing goods from them.

Prices and Estimates on Application.

Rubber Tubing.
PURE WHITE.

MADE with Corrugated or Smooth Surface, and with walls $\frac{1}{16}$, (= "light"); $\frac{3}{32}$, (= "heavy"); and $\frac{1}{8}$ inch, (= "extra heavy,") thick. Put up boxes containing 50 or 100 feet, and sold either by list nd discount or by the pound.

List Price Per Pound, $1.50.

LIST PRICES PER FOOT.

nt. Diam.	Per ft.	Int. Diam.	Per ft.
8 inch	$0.08	1/2 inch	$0.25
/16 "	.12	5/8 "	.30
/4 "	.16	3/4 "	.35
/16 "	.18	1 "	.45
/8 "	.20		

CLOTH INSERTION TUBING.

Iade usually in 12-foot Lengths, and sold by List and Discount.

nt. Diam.	Per ft.	Int. Diam.	Per ft.
/8 inch	$0.10	1/2 inch	$0.28
/16 "	.14	5/8 "	.33
/4 "	.18	3/4 "	.38
/16 "	.20	1 "	.50
/8 "	.23		

RUBBER TUBING—*Continued.*

Extra Heavy Beer Tubing.

With fine Para Rubber Lining, for brewers'
and bottlers' use.

Int. Diam.	Per ft.	Int. Diam.	Per ft.
1/4 inch	$0.18	5/8 inch	$0.3
5/16 "	.20	3/4 "	.3
3/8 "	.23	1 "	.5
1/2 "	.28		

Made to order, Red or Black Cover.

Fire Extinguisher and Soda Tubing.

RED, BLACK OR WHITE OUTSIDE.

Made extra strong and heavy, and of fine Para Rub
ber. Will stand very great pressure.

3/8 inch, inside diameter......... Per ft., 30c.

For Chemical Engine Hose, (see page 51).

Bicycle Pump Tubing.

RED OR WHITE OUTSIDE.

1/8 inch, inside diameter............... Per ft., 10c.

☞ Special Tubing for any other purpose made
to order at short notice.

Gas Tubing,   **Elevator Tubing,**

    Shaft Tubing,   **Acid Tubing**

Prices on Application.

RUBBER WATER HOSE.

For List Prices see page 37.

WE make Rubber Water Hose regularly in all sizes and plies, in two qualities described below. Garden Hose, being used only in two sizes. iz. : 1/2 and 3/4 inch is made by us in a much larger ariety of grades, described separately on pages 38 to 40.

"MALTESE CROSS" brand of Water Hose.— A very superior grade made to meet the demand for a ong service hose. It is high priced, but is well worth ts cost, and cheapest in the long run. All the materials mployed in its construction are selected, and heavier luck used to give it greater strength and durability.

"LION" brand of Water Hose.—This brand is so well-known and extensively used throughout the Dominion as to scarcely need description. Its unequalled record for ten years as the best **standard** hose on the market, has caused its adoption by railways, steamers, factories, farms and the hardware, plumbing and mill supply trade generally. We carry in stock all usual sizes and plies, from 1/2 to 2 1/2 inch inclusive.

For List Prices see page 37.

INFORMATION REGARDING RUBBER WATER HOSE.

The **strength** of hose lies in the **cotton fabric or Duck.** This we prepare **expressly** to accommodate the pressure required. The higher the pressure and the larger the size of hose the greater should be the number of plies ordered.

2-PLY HOSE.—Used only for **conducting** water under moderate pressure. The larger sizes are used for Railway Tanks and Depot purposes.

3-PLY HOSE.—Intended for **Hydrant, Garden** and **Force Pump** uses, where the pressure does not exceed 75 lbs per square inch.

4-PLY HOSE.—Recommended particularly in sizes larger than 1 inch for all general purposes; also in the smaller sizes where pressure is very heavy or service severe. By increasing the number of plies the strength and durability of the hose is increased.

For List Price see page 37.

LIST PRICES FOR ALL KINDS OF

Rubber Water & Garden Hose.

☞These list prices apply to all grades of Rubber Water Hose, the discounts from these list prices varying according to quality.

☞The size of any hose is determined by the inside diameter. In ordering, specify **size, number of plies and grade wanted.**

Interior Diameter.	2 Ply. per foot.	3 Ply. per foot.	4 Ply. per foot.
1/2 inch	$0.20	$0.25	$0.30
3/4 "	.25	.30	.37
1 "	.33	.40	.50
1 1/4 "	.42	.50	.62
1 1/2 "	.50	.60	.75
1 3/4 "	.58	.70	.87
2 "	.66	.80	1.00
2 1/4 "	.75	.90	1.12
2 1/2 "	.83	1.00	1.25
2 3/4 "	.92	1.10	1.37
3 "	.99	1.20	1.50
3 1/2 "	1.15	1.40	1.75
4 "	1.32	1.60	2.00
5 "	1.65	2.00	2.50
6 "	1.98	....	....
7 "	2.31	....	....
8 "	2.64	....	....
9 "	2.97	....	....
10 "	3.33	....	....

Five or six-ply Hose made at an advance of 25 and 50 per cent. respectively on four-ply prices.

Intermediate sizes charged at the list price of the next larger size, thus: ⅞-inch will be charged at 1-inch price, etc.

GARDEN HOSE.

(For List Prices see page 37).

TO meet the requirements of the trade we manufacture Garden Hose in several different grades, varying in price according to the quality. We append a short description of some of the best known brands, of which we alway carry a large quantity in stock.

All our fine grades of hose are **hand made**, with **double tube.** We are the original makers also in Canada of **machine made Seamless Tube Hose** and can supply it where required.

When hose leaks **don't wrap a rag around it,** but **cut out the bad place** and join the two ends together with a mender or coupling. More hose is destroyed through not doing this than in any other way.

We describe below our principal brands.

"MALTESE CROSS" Brand. (Not Carbolized Fire Hose).—This, our best brand, we offer as the finest garden hose made. Those who desire, and are willing to pay a fair price for a really superior article will find this the most economical hose to purchase.

Usual sizes always in stock, others made to order on short notice.

"EXTRA FINE" Brand.—This we offer as an article of actual extra quality at moderate cost. A trial of this brand will prove its merits, and we will cheerfully replace any defective lengths should such be found.

"WHITE" (extra quality) **HOSE.**

"RED" (Antimony) **HOSE.**

The natural color of hose made from fine quality rubber is **black** or **grey ;** other colors may be obtained by compounding with foreign ingredients, but a **better quality** can always be made at a given price in the **natural color.** For those who wish colored hose we make our **"Extra Quality White"** and **"Antimony"** (red) brands.

GARDEN HOSE—*Continued.*

LION" **Brand.**—This is the popular grade. We guarantee it to give entire satisfaction for all ordinary purposes, and its extraordinary record during the past ten (10) years has caused this brand to be accepted as **the standard** by the trade generally. When quality is not specified we always fill orders with the "**Lion**" brand of hose.

All sizes from 1/2 to 2 1/2 inch of this grade kept constantly in stock.

KING " **Brand.**—This is a good grade of hose for lawn purposes, at a moderate price. Made regularly in 3/4 and 1/2 inch 3 ply only.

LEADER " **Brand.**—A low priced hose for service where the pressure is not very great, though it is frequently sold for ordinary lawn purposes. Made regularly in 3/4 and 1/2 inch 3 ply sizes only.

COMPETITION " **Brand.**—The cheapest hose we make. Not recommended for severe service, it will, however, be found to be of much better material than is usually put in cheap hose sold under this or similar brand. Made regularly in 3/4 inch and 1/2 inch 3 ply sizes only.

COTTON GARDEN HOSE.

"**FAIRY**" **Brand.**—For those who prefer Cotton-rubber-lined hose we can recommend this brand as positively the best in the market. Cotton hose should always be **thoroughly dried after use,** and kept on a hose reel.

Kept in stock in 1/2, 3/4 and 1 inch sizes.

List Prices same as 3-Ply Rubber Hose, see page 37.

5

GARDEN HOSE—*Continued.*

"KINKPROOF" (Copyrighted) Brand.

STEEL CLAD ARMOURED HOSE.

The Most Perfect Wire Bound Hose Manufactured.

By means of our new Murphy's Patent Wiring Machine, for the use of which we have the sole rights in Canada, we are enabled to supply Armoured or Wire-Wound Hose that is free from all the defects of Wire-Wound Hose heretofore offered. The "**Kinkproof**" Hose may be cut at any wind of the wire without loosening or uncoiling; the wire being **self-gripping** throughout its entire length.

Will Resist Practically Unlimited Pressure.

The Wire Armour is an efficient protection against abrasion for Mining, Air, Acid, Green House, Lawn, Livery Stable, Brewers, Tanners, Oil, and Wrecking Hose, and for all purposes where Hose is subjected to rough, hard usage. Building Contractors will find the "**Kinkproof**" Hose most valuable for their service.

We wire any Hose up to three inches in diameter to order.

"**Kinkproof**" Garden Hose is sold on the regular water hose list.

For List Prices see page 37.

GARDEN HOSE SUNDRIES.
"JIM DANDY" REELS.

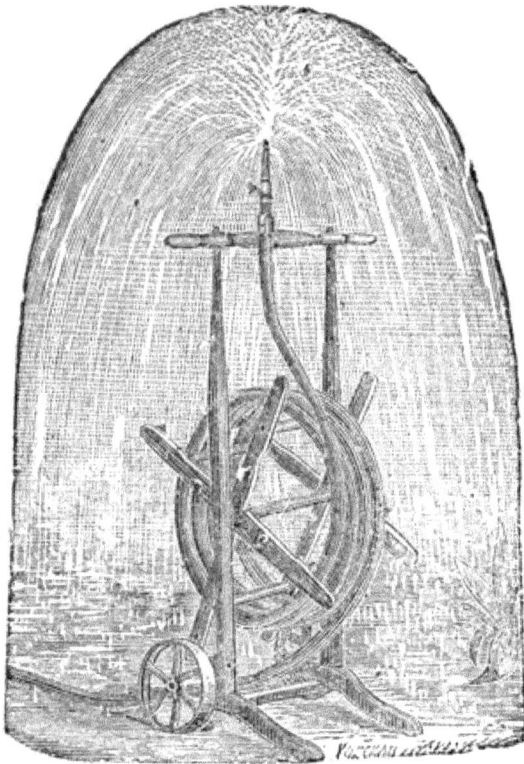

Capacity 100 ft. of 3-4 Hose.

We have these reels made to our own special design, of better materials, and stronger than the ordinary cheap Reels. At the low price we offer them, no one using lawn hose can afford to be without one. Will pay for themselves in one season's use in saving of hose.

Best lawn hose reel on the market at anything like the cost.

List Price, Per Dozen, $12.00.

Garden Hose Sundries—*Continued.*

COUPLINGS.--Brass, Shank Pattern.

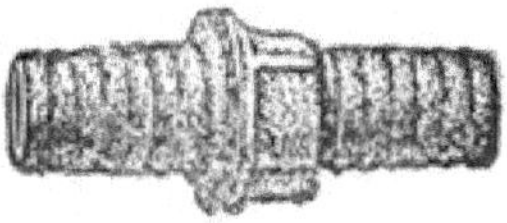

Size.		Per doz. For Water—Hose.	Per doz. Steam Hose long Shanks
1/2	inch Couplings, Hose thread	$2.40	$4.80
3/4	" " " "	2.40	4.80
1	" " " "	4.40	9.00
1 1/4	" " Iron Pipe thread	10.00	15.00
1 1/2	" " " "	14 00	24.00
2	" " " "	24.00	.....
2 1/2	" " " "	48.00	.....
3	" " " "	76.00	....

"CALDWELL" HOSE BANDS.

Simplest Appliance for Attaching Couplings to Lawn Hose.

Size of Hose,	1/2 in.	3/4 in.	1 in.	1 1/4 in.	1 1/2 in.
Bands, per gross .	$4.80	$7.20	$9.60	$12.00	$14.40
Pliers, per doz ...	7.00	7.00	9.00	9.00	.....

"HUDSON" HOSE MENDERS.

For repairing damaged Lawn Hose.

Size of Hose,	1/2 in.	3/4 in.	1 in.
Bands, per gross	$3.00	$3.60	......
Thimbles, per gross............	4.80	6.00	.....
Pliers, per doz	5.00	5.00	......

Garden Hose Sundries—*Continued.*

"SQUEEZER NOZZLES"—Rubber.

Specially adapted for sprinkling plants and washing vehicles.

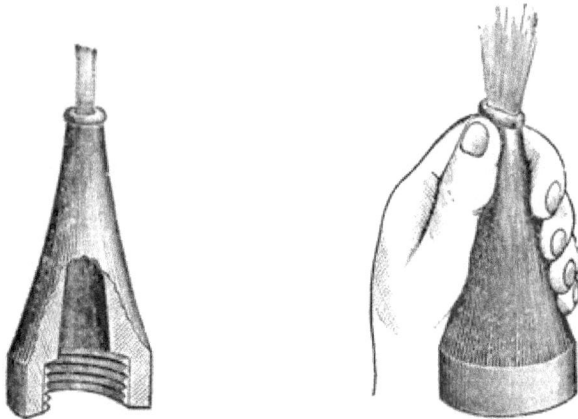

For 1/2 and 3/4 inch Hose only.

Made entirely of Rubber they are not injured by falling, and cannot get out of order.

To produce a Spray or Shut Off, simply compress or "Squeeze" the soft rubber tip between the thumb and forefinger, as shown in cut. **Price, per doz., - $7.00**

'GUTTA PERCHA' NOZZLE—Brass. (For 1/2 and 3/4 inch Hose only). This is a **controlling nozzle** of our special design and will throw Solid Stream or Spray, and will **shut off** completely by simply revolving the sleeve. Thoroughly reliable and satisfactory.

> **Polished Brass,** 1/2 and 3/4 in....per doz. $12.00
> **Nickel Plated,** " " .... " 15.00

'C.L.E." NOZZLES—Brass. With screw tip and stop cock on large end. Throws Solid Stream only, and will Shut Off. When Spray Stream is wanted a brass **rose** may be order, (extra charge), and screwed on in place of the tip.

> **Polished Brass,** 1/2 and 3/4 in....per doz. $12.00
> " " 1 in .... " 20.00

"PLAIN" NOZZLES — Brass — Without cock or separating tip, made in all sizes up to 2 1/2 in. and varying in length. **Prices upon application.**

RUBBER WASHERS.

HOSE WASHERS.

Size for Lawn Hose	-		1/2 in.	3/4 in.	1 in.
Per Gross	-	-	-	$1.50	1.50	3.00

Size	-	1 1/4 in.	1 1/2 in.	1 3/4 in.	2 in.	2 1/4 in.
Per Doz.	-	.75	1.00	1.25	1.50	1.75

All Above Sizes.......... ....per lb, $2.50.

FIRE AND SUCTION HOSE WASHERS.

Size	-	-	2 1/2 in.	3 in.	3 1/2 in.	4 in.	4 1/2 in.
Per Doz.	-		$2.00	2.50	3.00	3.50	4.00

All Above Sizes..................per lb., $3.00.

Gauge Glass Washers.

Size of Glass	-	3/8 in.	1/2 in.	5/8 in.	3/4 in.	7/8 in.
Square, per Gross	$3.00	3.00	3.50	4.50	5.00
Round, "	4.00	4.00	4.50	5.00	5.50

All Above Sizes..................per lb., $2.50.

STEAM HOSE.

'MALTESE CROSS" Brand.—Made of the best quality Fine Para Rubber, and on Extra Heavy Duck. A superior article. Kept in stock in regular sizes.

SALAMANDER" Brand.—Made on Extra Strong Duck and and a high grade of Rubber, second in quality to our "Maltese Cross" brand only. Made to order only.

"LION" Brand.—This is the popular grade, **and is what we always ship when higher priced grades are not specified.** A reliable article. Kept in stock, in all usual sizes.

Steam Hose, as ordinarily made, is **vulcanized** at a **temperature of 240°.** Therefore, whenever it is **subjected** to a continuous **heat greater** than **240°,** the rubber is hardened and the **hose will deteriorate.**

We append a table of the heat generated by steam pressure, from which consumers will see the advantage of keeping the steam pressure below 40 lbs.

```
40 lbs. steam pressure generates............269° heat.
50  "      "       "       "      ..............283°  "
60  "      "       "       "      ............ ....295°  "
70  "      "       "       "      .... ..... ..306°  "
80  "      "       "       "      ............ .315°  "
90  "      "       "       "      .......... ....321°  "
100  "      "       "       "      ..............332°  "
```

For List Prices see page 46

STEAM HOSE—*Continued.*

Int. Diam.	3-Ply. Based on 20 lbs steam 1 in. hose. per ft.	4-Ply. Based on 35 lbs steam 1 in. hose. per ft.	5-Ply. Based on 50 lbs steam 1 in. hose per ft.	6-Ply. Based on 75 lbs steam 1 in. hose. per ft.
1/2 inch.......	$0.43	$0.51	$0.63	$0.76
3/4 "	.51	.67	.83	1.00
1 "	.67	.83	1.03	1.24
1 1/4 "	.85	1.04	1.30	1.56
1 1/2 "	1.02	1.25	1.56	1.87
1 3/4 "	1.18	1.45	1.81	2.17
2 "	1.34	1.66	2.07	2.49
2 1/2 "	1.66	2.08	2.60	3.12
3 "	2.00	2.80	3.50	4.20

For each additional ply add 25 per cent. of 4-ply prices. Larger sizes made when required.

See pages 45 and 47.

MARLIN WOUND steam hose at 10 per cent. advance on above List prices.

WIRE WOUND steam hose at 12 per cent. advance on above List Prices. All our wiring is warranted not to unwind when cut.

AIR DRILL HOSE.

ᗰ ADE in two styles as per cuts herewith. Each style is also made in two qualities viz : **"Maltese Cross"** and **"Lion" brands.**

Tough, durable rubber is used and strong duck to withstand tremendous pressure and resist wear and tear for a long time.

This cut shows the **canvas cover** style, the outer covering being of canvas and counting as 1 ply in the list price.

This cut shows the **wire wound** or **"kink-proof"** style. The wire increases the strength and protects the hose from being cut on sharp rocks. For this style add 12 per cent. to List Prices below.

All our wiring is warranted not to unwind when cut.

List Prices for all Styles and Qualities of Air Drill Hose.

Size Inside Diameter.	4-Ply. 3-ply inside and 1-ply outside.	5-Ply. 4-ply inside and 1-ply outside.	6-Ply. 5-ply inside and 1-ply outside.
3/4 inch............	$0.67	$0.83	$1.00
1 "	0.83	1.03	1.24
1 1/4 "	1.04	1.30	1.56
1 1/2 "	1.25	1.56	1.87
1 3/4 "	1.45	1.81	2.17
2 "	1.66	2.07	2.49
2 1/2 "	2.08	2.60	3.12
3 "	2.80	3.50	4.20

If served with **Marlin** add 10 per cent to these List Prices.

N.B.—For list prices of **Steam Hose for Rock Drills,** either Plain or Marlin wound, or wire wound, see list prices page 46.

6

BREWERS' HOSE.

T HIS hose is made specially to meet the requirements of Brewers' use, and is **warranted not to kink.**
The lining is made of a gum intended to resist the action of steam and hot liquids without imparting a disagreeable taste or smell. The rubber cover is made heavy to resist hard service. We make three grades, viz.:—

"Maltese Cross" brand.—A superior quality unexcelled for the purpose, kept in stock in the regular sizes.

"Crescent" brand.—An extra quality at medium price. Made to order only.

"Lion" brand.—The popular, standard grade. We usually fill orders with this grade when no brand is specified. Kept in stock in the regular sizes.

N.B.—**Customers will confer a favor by specifying by name, on their orders, the brand wanted.**

Int. Diam.	3 Ply. per ft.	4 Ply. per ft.	Int. Diam.	3 Ply. per ft.	4 Ply. per ft.
1/2 in........	$0.43	$0.51	1 3/4 in....	$1.18	$1.45
3/4 "	.51	.67	2 "	1.34	1.66
1 "	.67	.83	2 1/2 "	1.66	2.08
1 1/4 "	.85	1.04	3 "	2.00	2.80
1 1/2 "	1.02	1.25			

FIVE AND SIX PLY BREWERS' HOSE.

made at an advance of 25 and 50 per cent. respectively on 4-ply prices.

Served with wire on the outside at 12 per cent. advance on list prices.

All hose wired by us is warranted not to unwind when cut.

OIL HOSE.

"Maltese Cross" and "Lion" Brands.

(Not kept in stock but made to order
on short notice).

Made with a **tube** and **cover specially prepared
under** a **process** known **only to ourselves,**
and the *only* Hose that will **successfully** withstand
the action of **Petroleum** and **other oils. Every section of the** "Maltese Cross" **brand bears our
trade mark as above.**

THREE-PLY. FOUR-PLY.

Int. Diam.	Per ft.	Int. Diam.	Per ft.
1/2 inch	$0.43	1/2 inch	$0.51
3/4 "	.51	3/4 "	.67
1 "	.67	1 "	.83
1 1/4 "	.85	1 1/4 "	1.04
1 1/2 "	1.02	1 1/2 "	1.25
1 3/4 "	1.18	1 3/4 "	1.45
2 "	1.34	2 "	1.66
2 1/2 "	1.66	2 1/2 "	2.08
3 "	2.00	3 "	2.80

For each additional ply add 25 per cent. of four-ply
prices.

Larger sizes made when required.

Served with Marlin at 10 per cent., or with Wire at
12 per cent. advance on list prices.

All our wiring is warranted not to unwind when cut.

**Oil Suction Hose, on Spiral Wire, made to
order upon application.**

AIR-BRAKE HOSE.

FOR RAILWAY USE.

50-Foot Lengths.

1 inch 4 ply int. diam . . . . $0.83 per foot.
1 1/4 " 4 " " " . . . . 1.04 "
1 1/2 " 4 " " " . . . . 1.25 "

20 to 24 Inch Lengths.

(ENDS CAPPED AND ENLARGED).

1   inch 4 ply int. diam . . . . $2.00 per length.
1 1/4 " 4 " " " . . . . 2.50 "

WESTINGHOUSE BRAKE WASHERS.

Per Pound. . . $2.50.

VACUUM BRAKE HOSE.

Corrugated.

Plain.

Made with enlarged ends, either corrugated or plain
upon the best Bessemer steel wire in

20 to 24 Inch Lengths.

1   inch int. diam. . . . . $2.40 per length.
1 1/4 " " " . . . . 3.00 "

DIAPHRAGMS FOR VACUUM BRAKES.

All Sizes.
PRICES UPON APPLICATION.

CHEMICAL ENGINE HOSE.

"Maltese Cross" and "Lion" brands.

This Hose is specially made to resist the action of Chemical Engine charges. It also combines great strength and pliability without the tendency to kink.

The "Maltese Cross" brand is without equal for Fire Department Service.

_____

LIST PRICES.

3/4 inch, 4 ply	per ft.	$0.67
1 " "	"	.83
1 1/4 " "	"	1.04

_____

For Fire Extinguisher Tubing see page 34.

_____

DIVERS' HOSE.

"Maltese Cross" brand.

We make regularly but one quality of Divers' Hose, and that the best. It is intended to float when in service, and is specially made to prevent kinking and chafing, and to withstand the action of either fresh or salt water. It is also compounded to prevent imparting a disagreeable odor to the air supplied through it to the Diver.

_____

LIST PRICES.

1/2 inch, 4 ply	per ft.	$0.51
3/4 " "	"	.67

SUCTION HOSE—"Plain Spiral."
"Maltese Cross," "Crescent" and "Lion" Brands.

ON SPIRAL BRASS WIRE.

Int. Diam.	Per ft.	Int. Diam.	Per ft.
3/4 inch	$0.77	1 1/2 inch	$1.65
1 "	1.00	1 3/4 "	2.10
1 1/4 "	1.25	2 "	2.50

ON SPIRAL TINNED OR STEEL WIRE.

Int. Diam.	Per ft.	Int. Diam.	Per ft.
3/4 inch	$0.70	1 1/2 inch	$1.50
1 "	.90	1 3/4 "	1.90
1 1/4 "	1.15	2 "	2.30

Large sizes of Plain Spiral Suction Hose for **wrecking, mining, dredging, etc.,** are made to order on Flat or Round Galvanized Bessemer Steel Wire, wound spirally according to size and length required. Our Suction is unequalled for its flexibility and durable qualities.

2 1/4 inch	$2.70	6 inch	$9.50
2 1/2 "	3.10	6 1/2 "	10.50
3 "	4.00	7 "	12.00
3 1/2 "	4.90	7 1/2 "	13.50
4 "	5.80	8 "	15.00
4 1/2 "	6.70	9 "	17.50
5 "	7.60	10 "	20.00
5 1/2 "	8.50	12 "	25.00

Orders executed on short notice.
SUCTION HOSE FOR OIL REFINERS A SPECIALTY.

SUCTION HOSE—"Smooth Bore."

"Maltese Cross," "Crescent" and "Lion" Brands.

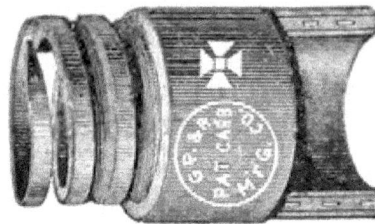

This style is far superior to the ordinary suction hose, and is now almost invariably used on **Fire Engines.** The Galvanized steel coil being securely enclosed in smooth rubber walls, it is thereby protected from the action of water passing through it, and the friction occasioned by the rough inside surface of ordinary suction is entirely avoided, and consequently a very much greater volume of water obtained.

Int. Diam.	Per ft.	Int. Diam.	Per ft.
2 inch	$2.60	6 inch	$10.50
2 1/2 "	3.50	6 1/2 "	12.00
3 "	4.50	7 "	13.50
3 1/2 "	5.50	7 1/2 "	15.00
4 "	6.50	8 "	16.50
4 1/2 "	7.50	9 "	19.50
5 "	8.50	10 "	22.50
5 1/2 "	9.50	12 "	27.50

The **"Maltese Cross" Brand** of both Plain Spiral and Smooth Bore Suction Hose is "carbolized," as explained below, and the Smooth Bore is unequalled for Fire Department service.

The rubber and duck used in the manufacture of this Suction are treated under our **secret carbolizing process,** in the same manner as our **"Maltese Cross" Brand Fire Hose,** and is thereby effectually preserved from mildew and rot. The '**Maltese Cross Carbolized" Brand** will outwear any Suction Hose on earth.

"Agricultural" Suction Hose.

Light, with Spiral Wire imbedded.
for Agricultural Pumps.

1 1/4 inch.....per ft. $0.93		2 inch.....per ft. $1.50		
1 1/2 " ..... " 1.13		2 1/4 " ..... " 1.69		
1 3/4 " ..... " 1.31		2 1/2 " ..... " 1.88		

"KINKPROOF" SUCTION HOSE.

For Threshing Engines.

With Spiral Wire outside to prevent collapsing, kinking or chafing. Cheap and efficient.

3 PLY.	4 PLY.
1/2 inch ....per ft. $0.25	1/2 inch....per ft. $0.30
3/4 " ..... " .30	3/4 " ..... " .37
1 " ..... " .40	1 " ..... " .50

Made in 50 ft. sections.   May be cut at any point without the wire unwinding or springing loose.

HARD RUBBER SUCTION HOSE.

"CRESCENT" and "LION" BRANDS.

This Suction Hose is intended for **Pumps** and **Steam Threshing Engines.** It will not collapse, and will be found a reliable and durable article for the purposes to which it is suited.

Int. Diam.	Int. Diam.
3/4 inch ....per ft. $0.65	1 3/4 inch.....per ft. $1.31
1 " ..... " 0.75	2 " ..... " 1.50
1 1/4 " ... " 0.93	2 1/4 " ..... " 1.69
1 1/2 " ..... " 1.13	2 1/2 " ..... " 1.88

Not recommended in the larger sizes except for light service.

"Maltese Cross" Brand, Patent Carbolized
FLEXIBLE RUBBER PLAY PIPES.

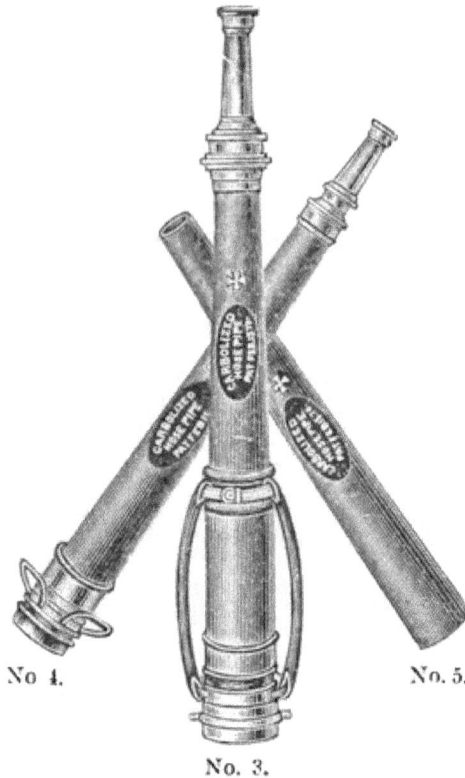

No 4.   No. 5.

No. 3.

Best Fire Department Pipe made, 2½ inches internal diameter at the butt, and about 33 inches long, with fittings complete.

PRICES:

Nos. 1, 2 and 3, with Brass Fittings and Leather Handles, complete	$20.00
No 4, with Brass Handles and Fittings	18.00
No. 5, without Fittings	10.00
Nos. 6 and 7, with straight tubes	20.00

The great strength and flexibility of our "MALTESE CROSS" PIPES and their superiority over the Brass Pipes formerly used, is too well known to need comment. Hard knocks will not dent them.

HEAVY BRASS SERVICE PIPES.

These pipes are substantially made and are for Fire Dept., or Mill Service. Made with screw nozzles and with or without handles.

Price, Each.................................$10.00

We also have cheaper Brass Pipes.

"MALTESE CROSS" BRAND

Carbolized Rubber Fire Hose.

Unrivalled Record Extending over Twenty-five Years.

The strongest and most durable Fire Hose in the World.

Manufactured under letters patent.

Absolutely Mildew and Rot Proof. The only Hose that need not be dried after use and will not rot. Made in three weights, all at same price, 50, 55 or 65 lbs. to the 50-foot Section.

Samples, Prices and special Fire Department Catalogue furnished upon application.

Over six million feet sold under a three years' guarantee, and less than one quarter of one per cent. returned to be replaced. We are the only manufacturers in the world who can make a 50 lb. Rubber Hose that will withstand successfully the wear and tear of Fire service. The **"Maltese Cross"** Fire Hose is now used in over 1,000 Fire Departments.

THE VALUE OF THE
CARBOLIZING TREATMENT
OF OUR
"MALTESE CROSS" HOSE
is illustrated below in a striking manner.

This cut represents a piece of cotton duck such as we use in making hose.

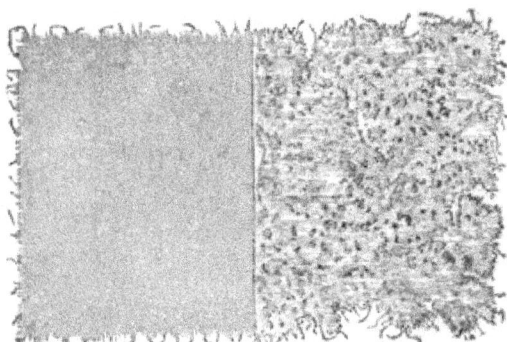

One-half was treated with our patent Carbolizing Solution. The whole was then buried in a damp, muddy soil for six weeks. When taken out that portion of the duck which had been treated with our solution was found to be perfectly sound, while the portion not carbolized was entirely destroyed by rot.

Being mildew and rot proof, it need not be dried after use, and therefore but one line of hose is necessary. No expensive tower or other apparatus for drying is needed. Save the money required for a tower and a double supply of hose, and invest in our "MALTESE CROSS," that needs no drying.

If interested write for Testimonials.

NOTE.—We also make the "Crescent" and "Beaver" brands of Rubber Fire Hose, lower in price than the "Maltese Cross."

"BAKER FABRIC"
COTTON FIRE HOSE.

Re-Inforced Rubber Lining.

Solid Multiple Woven.

The most Pliable and Strongest Cotton Hose in the World.

Possesses more points of advantage in its construction, and is the most popular brand of Cotton Rubber-Lined Fire Hose in the market.

Equally Flexible Wet or Dry.

Woven of **hard twisted cords**, it presents the best possible wearing surface, and will absorb less water or mud, and will therefore **dry quicker** than other brands which are made of loose, fluffy yarns.

Samples, Prices and Special Fire Dep't. Catalogue furnished on application.

Ours is the only Cotton Fire Hose in which the patent re-inforced linings can be used.

NOTE.—We also manufacture many other brands of Cotton Fire Hose, including "Jacket" or Double Hose and "Knitted" Hose.

The "Baker Fabric" Cotton Fire Hose

is woven *flat*, and therefore, when reeled, is in its *natural* position ; an important fact which should be kept in view when comparing it with circular woven hose ; the latter, when reeled, is subjected to great strain on the edges or folds of the coil, necessarily weakening the fabric, and causing its premature decay. This is evidenced by the fact that circular woven hose usually bursts along the line of the folds, where the fabric has been strained and distorted in reeling. **The "Baker Fabric" Hose is free from this defect.**

This Hose is woven of any number of plies necessary to suit the pressure to be resisted. **And a most valuable feature of the weave is, that the whole outer ply may be cut or worn away, without affecting the strength of the plies beneath. Therefore, if in a four-ply hose, the outer ply be destroyed, the effective strength of a three-ply hose remains.** Also, owing to the manner of weaving this tubular fabric, the hose will unreel straight, and not *writhe* or *twist* under pressure. It is equally soft and pliable, *wet* or *dry*. **The Fabric is treated with an antiseptic, rendering it absolutely mildew-proof and is so guaranteed.** In weaving this Fabric, we produce an exterior of coarse, strong yarns offering greater resistance to the wear and tear resulting from the use of the hose, while the interior is constructed of finer threads, in order to present a smooth surface to the rubber lining. **When lined, it has a perfectly smooth water-way, which reduces the friction to a minimum.** Firemen and engineers will appreciate this advantage, because in hose having a corrugated interior surface, a large percentage of the power of the engine is lost in overcoming frictional resistance. This is an advantage possessed by the **"Baker Fabric"** alone, all other brands of Cotton Fire Hose having a rough interior surface.

The patents under which **The "Baker Fabric" Hose** is manufactured have been subjected to the closest scrutiny, and received the unanimous endorsement of the *Honorable Board* of Examiners-in-Chief, March 5th, 1876.

Samples, Prices, and Special Information
Cheerfully Furnished.

"AJAX" BRAND

OF

RUBBER-LINED COTTON HOSE.

STRONG AND DURABLE.

FOR { FIRE DEPARTMENTS.
{ FACTORIES, MILLS, ETC.

The "Ajax" brand of hose may be relied upon as excellent value. It must not be confused with the very cheap, inferior grades of Cotton Hose. The different sizes are made to withstand pressures of from 300 to 400 lbs. The rubber linings are made of the same fine quality as used in our best brands of Fire Dep't Cotton Hose, than which no more reliable and durable are made.

LIST PRICES.

1 1/4 inch diameter ....per ft.			$0.48
1 1/2 " " .... "			0.53
2 " " .... "			0.65
2 1/4 " " .... "			0.70
2 1/2 " " Fire Department Size ... "			0.75

NOTE—We manufacture many brands and grades of Fire Hose in addition to those mentioned herein, including all styles "Multiple Woven," "Jacket," "Knitted," etc. Prices and information on application.

"U. S." BRAND.

Underwriters' Standard Cotton Fire Hose.

THE destinctive marks of this brand are **red, white and blue lines, woven the entire length of every section along one side.**

The "**U.S.**" is a very strong, light and durable **Cotton Fire Hose**, constructed especially to comply with the pecifications and requirements of Mr. John R. Freeaan, Hydraulic Engineer and Inspector of the Assoiated Factory Mutual Fire Insurance Companies, and acepted and approved as **the standard** by the inspectrs of these Companies.

The "**U. S.**" is well adapted for small Fire Dep'ts vhere it is not deemed advisable to purchase a higherriced hose. It will be found perfectly reliable if used a connection with Steam Fire Engines or direct water vorks pressure, though, of course, for heavy Fire Dep't iervice we would recommend as more suitable, one of ur heavier brands of **multiple woven hose**, or our 'Maltese Cross" brand rubber hose. **The latter s without an equal for hard service and great lurability.**

LINEN FIRE HOSE.

"THISTLE" BRAND.

Orange and Black Striped. Guaranteed.

Made to conform to the standard and requirements of the New England Mutual Fire Insurance Underwriters, from the most carefully selected yarns, and capable of resisting tremendous pressure. **Absolutely the best Linen Hose made.**

In process of weaving, the yarns are beaten up hard, so that in service the first contact with water causes the fibre to swell and renders the hose **almost absolutely water-tight** under any working pressure.

Its compactness, lightness, and great strength commend it for use in Railway Stations, Hotels, Public Buildings and Factories, where it may be kept neatly folded in Swinging Hose Racks.

Made in 2 1/2 inch, or Fire Department size only. Never made with rubber lining.

Samples, Prices and Further Information
on Application.

RUBBER FIRE BUCKETS.

Will not Break or Dent.

Per Dozen, - - - - $36.00.

LINEN HOSE—Unlined.

"Red and Blue Stripe" Brand.

Made in 50 ft. Lengths or Multiples thereof.

This Hose we stock in a **good quality** at low price, but we neither keep nor offer the **cheapest grades** in which Linen Hose is made, as we consider them unreliable.

1 inch diam............ ....per ft.	20	cents
1 1/4 " ... . "	24	"
1 1/2 " .... "	30	"
2 " .... "	36	"
2 1/4 " .... "	40	"
2 1/2 " .... "	45	"

Liberal Discount to the Trade.

LINEN HOSE—Rubber Lined.

Seamless, and made only in 50 Lengths.

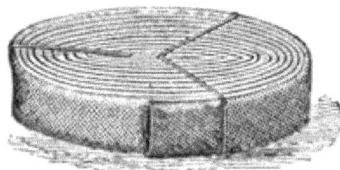

1 1/4 inch diam............................per ft.	48	cents
1 1/2 " .... "	53	"
2 " .... "	65	"
2 1/4 " .... "	70	"
2 1/2 " Fire Dep't Size .... "	75	"

Liberal Discount to the Trade.

SWINGING HOSE RACKS.

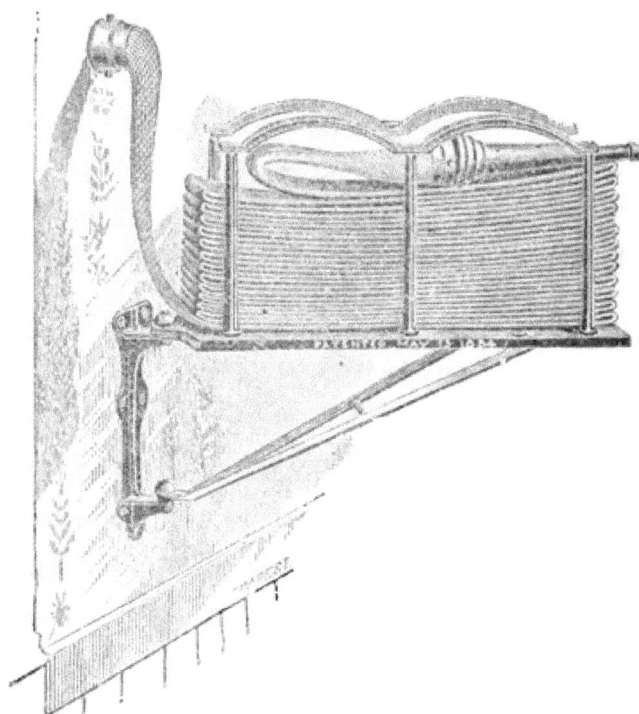

Made either with Brackets, as shown in cut, to attach to walls, or with Clamps to fit Stand Pipes.

Size and Kind.	Capacity.	Price, each
No. 0. for 1 1/2 or 2 inch, unlined......	50 ft.	$2.25
No. 00. " 2 1/2 inch, "	50 "	2.25
No. 1. " 1 1/2 or 2 inch, "	100 "	2.75
No. 2. " 2 1/2 inch, "	100 "	3.00
No. 3. " 1/2 or 2 inch, "	150 "	3.00
or 2 1/2 inch, rubber lined......	50 "	3.00
No. 4. for 2 1/2 inch, "	50 "	3.00
or 2 1/2 inch, unlined..........	150 "	3.00
No. 5. for 1 1/2 or 2 inch, rubber-lined..	100 "	4.00
No. 6. " 2 1/2 inch, " ..	100 "	4.50

**Prices include either Wall Brackets
or Clamps.**

HOSE JUMPERS---BALANCED.

STYLE "A."

Capacity 500 ft. 2½ Rubber or Cotton Hose.

EQUIPMENT.—Fifty feet of Drag Rope, Rope Reel, Pipe Holder, Tool Box, Wrenches, Sarven Wheels, Iron Frame and Forging, Steel Axle, painted English Vermillion and Striped, 5 ft. 2 in. wheels.

List Price.. .... $100.00

HOSE JUMPERS.

STYLE "B."

Capacity 250 or 300 feet, 2 1/2 inch "Maltese Cross"
Rubber Hose, or 400 feet Cotton Mill Hose.

This is a plain, substantial Cart, at low cost, suitable
for Mills, Warehouse and small Fire Departments.

List price,   -   -   -   - $75.00.

For more elaborate and higher priced Hose carts,
see our special Fire Department Catalogue.

PLUMBERS' SUPPLIES.

WATER CLOSET CONNECTIONS.

"Twyford's" Cup.   ·   "Conical."

"Demarest Floor Flange."

"Elbow Connections."

"Twyford's" Cup, 1 1/4 inch.... ....per doz. $5.00
    "   " 1 1/2 " .. ..   "   6.50
    "   " 2   " ....   "   9.00
" Elbow " Connections, 1 1/4 inch ....   "   9.00
"Conical " Connections, 1 1/4 inch ....   "   3.00
    "   "   1 1/2 " ....   "   3.60
" Demarest " Floor Flanges made of extra
   fine soft rubber ....   "   3.00

**Special moulded articles of any design
for Plumbers' use.**

RUBBER MATTING Corrugated.

Made in rolls about 30 yards long. and cut to order
in any size or shape desired.

Stock width 1 yard.   Narrower widths made to order.

List Price,   -   :   -   per lb., $0.50.

3/32 inches thick,	weighs about	7½ lbs. per square yard.
1/8 "	" "	10 " " "
3/16 "	" "	15 " " "
1/4 "	" "	19 " " "

This Matting is extensively used in the principal
hotels and public buildings throughout the country, both
for the **protection** of **stairs** and **carpets** indoors,
and for the **covering** of **verandas** outdoors.

It prevents **accidents** by slipping in **winter
weather,** and for use in places exposed to **wet** or
slush is **unrivalled.**   Its **wearing qualities** are
such that, under **ordinary circumstances,** it is
almost **indestructible.**

NO HOTEL SHOULD BE WITHOUT IT.

Stair Treads, of any size desired. cut to order from
Corrugated Matting.

NOTE—See page 73 for instructions re-laying this.

RUBBER MATS—Perforated.

Made to order of any **size, shape or thickness,** n a variety of patterns. Made also with **Solid Duck Back or Duck insertion**, when so ordered.

N.B.—In ordering irregular shaped Mats, send paper patterns, taking care to indicate thereon which is the upper side. Also indicate desired position of letters, if any.

Put your name on each pattern to avoid errors.

MADE IN TWO QUALITIES.

List Price, - - - - - per lb. $1.25.

Letters, 10c. each extra, net.

One square foot, 3/8 inch thick, weighs about two pounds.

Liberal Discount to the Trade.

RUBBER MATS—Corrugated.

SPECIAL SHAPE FOR
DENTISTS AND BARBERS.

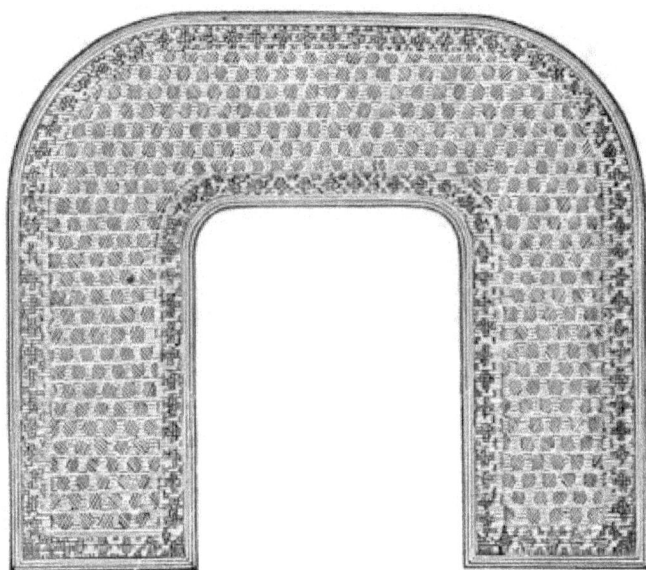

WE have frequently been asked for an attractive Mat to go around the Chairs of Dentists or Barbers, to **prevent noise** in some cases, to **save carpets** in others, and to provide a comfortable footing for those whose occupation compels them to stand on Tiled or Hardwood floors.

These Mats will meet the requirements. They are handsome in design, very durable and not very expensive. They are about 47 inches by 57 inches, outside measurement, with a tread 15 inches wide. Perforated Mats may also be made in the same shape.

3 3/2 inch thick . . . . per doz. $50.00.
1/8   "   "   . . . .   "   63.00.

RUBBER MATS.

DIAMOND PATTERNS.

NO. 1.

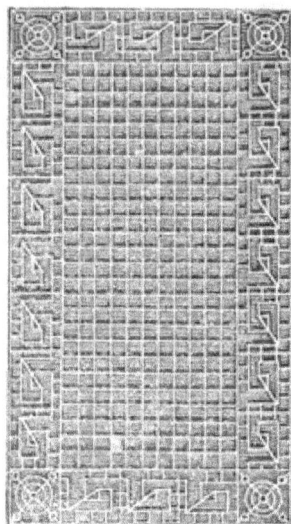

NO. 3.

NO. 2.

NO. 6.

For Description and Prices, see next page.

Rubber Mats—Miscellaneous.

No. 7.

Pitcher.

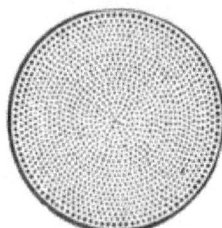

Coin.

Cuspidor Mat.

No.	1.	17x31 oval,	-	-	per dozen,	$27.00
"	2.	17x31	-	- - -	"	30.00
"	3.	17x31 with border,	-		"	30.00
"	6.	17x31 "	-	-	"	30.00
"	7.	17x31 "	-	-	"	30.00
Pitcher Mats, octagon			-	-	"	10.50
Coin	"	9 3/4 inches diameter,			"	9.00
Cuspidor	"	18x18 inches square	-		"	12.00

Rubber Mats—Corrugated.

Made about ⅛ inch thick, and in 2 patterns, viz., "A" and "D." Size about 17x31 inches.

This Cut Shows Pattern A.

Special sizes or varieties of pattern may be made if a quantity is required, but the cost of the necessary mould will have to be charged.

List Price for Patterns "A" and "D," per doz., $15.00

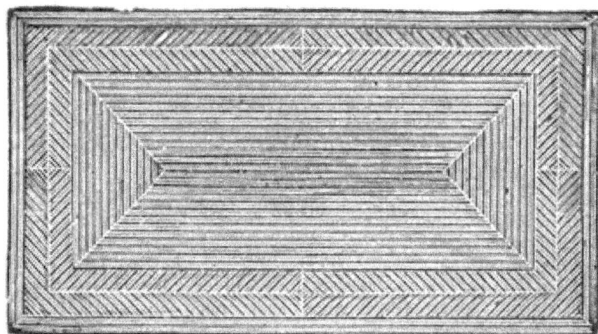

This Cut Shows Pattern D.

NOTE.—These Mats, as well as Corrugated Matting, may be **laid in GLUE** on the floor, or fastened with broad headed tacks.

Rubber Stair Treads--Moulded.

Cuts below show Patterns and Sizes kept in stock.

Pattern "A."

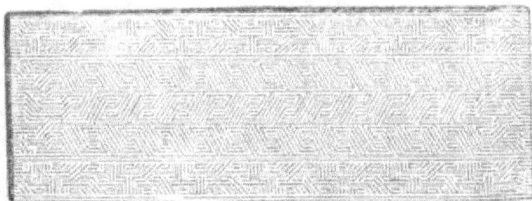

7" x 18"
9" x 48"

Pattern "B."

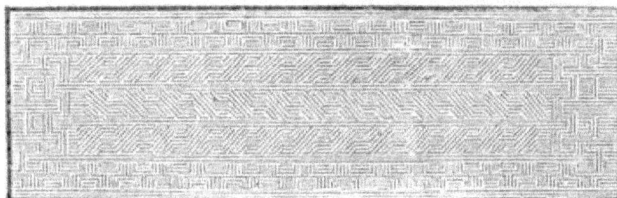

6 1/2" x 21".

Pattern "C."

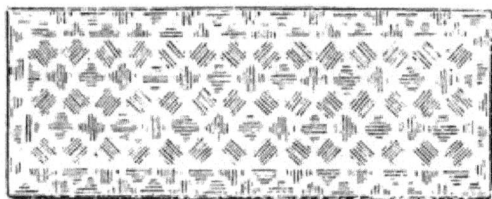

7 3/4" x 20 1/2".

Pattern "D."

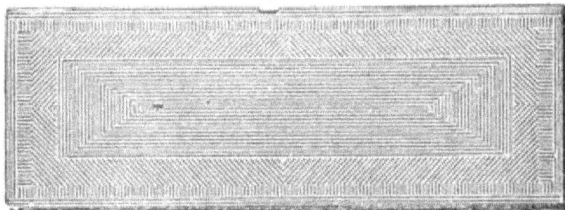

6 3/4" x 19 3/4".

"Dot" Pattern.

9" x 24"; 9" x 36".

NOTE.--As the thickness varies somewhat the weight also fluctuates.
Price per lb. - (any pattern), - **$0.60.**

METAL NOSINGS

FOR RUBBER STAIR TREADS.

Made to order in lengths desired. Not carried in stock.

Plain Pattern.

		ZINC.	BRASS.
1 1/4 in. wide	- -	$0.15	.30 per ft.

Fluted Pattern.

		ZINC.	BRASS.
1 1/4 in. wide	- -	$0.15	.30 per ft.

Embossed Pattern.

		ZINC.	BRASS.
1 1/4 in. wide	- -	$0.15	.30 per ft.

Subject to discount to the trade.

Special sizes made to order.

Pure Rubber Cement.

Bicycle Repair Cement.

(In Collapsible Tubes).

1/2 inch Tubes, - - - - - - per doz. $1.00	
3/4 " " - - - - - - " 1.50	
1 " " - - - - - - " 2.00	

Special Pure Rubber Cement.

(For Bicycle Tire Manufacturers).

We are prepared to contract for supplying this Cement in bulk, either in barrels or cans, to suit purchasers. Our Cement will be found of uniform quality, and is guaranteed to be the best it is possible to produce.

Pure Rubber Cement.

(For General Repair Work).

No. 3 (half-pints), - - - - - per doz. $ 4.00	
No. 2 (pints) - - - - - - " 7.00	
No. 1 (quarts), - - - - - " 12.00	
Per Gallon, - - - - - - 3.25	

BICYCLE TIRES.

We are prepared to manufacture Pneumatic Bicycle Tires, in any of the prevailing styles, for owners of patents thereof.

Special contracts for this work must be made with our Head Office.

BICYCLE INNER TUBES.

We are also prepared to manufacture the Pure Rubber Inner Tubes, used in "Double Tube" Tires.

Our products in this line are unexcelled for fine quality and finish. Our aim is not to supply the lowest priced article which may be produced, but with the finest materials and most improved methods of manufacture to turn out goods which cannot be surpassed.

The "PRIZE" Wringer.

PATENTED.

All White Rubber Rolls 11 x 1¾ inch.

INVISIBLE COGS.   AUTOMATIC CLAMPS.

Awarded First Prize at Worlds' Fair, Chicago, 1893
The Best, Simplest and most Durable Wringer made.

WISHING to offer our friends and customers the best Wringer obtainable, we have acquired the sole rights of manufacture and sale for Canada of the above machine, which was awarded the First Prize at World's Fair, Chicago, in 1893. The "Prize" is not offered as the lowest priced wringer on the market, but its fine quality, simplicity and great durability will prove it to be the cheapest in the long run. Our special facilities for manufacturing this wringer enable us to offer it at a very favorable price, but very little in advance of the ordinary cheap machines.

List Price, Per Dozen $48.00

The "PRIZE" Wringer.

(Continued.)

THE **Prize Wringer** commends itself on sight as the simplest, most efficient and durable wringer manufactured. It will wring perfectly the thinnest as well as the thickest material without turning the thumb-screw to change the pressure, or making any other alterations in the machine. **Fitted with best white rubber rolls vulcanized to shaft.** Made of best malleable iron, galvanized so that it cannot rust, and will not break with rough handling.

It is superior to all other wringers in construction, and stands without a rival in the rapidity and ease with which it may be attached and removed from the tub. One movement of the lever at the top does it all. No thumb-screws to turn or get out of order; has all the advantages of cog wringers, and overcomes all objections raised against them.

The only Wringer in which there can be no pressure on the Rolls or tension on the Springs when not in use.—Two very important features.

WRINGER ROLLS.

TABLE OF REGULAR SIZES IN STOCK.

Length.	Outside Diameter.	Size of Hole.
10 inch.........	1 1/2 inch.........	1/2 inch.........
10 "	1 5/8 "	1/2 " ....
10 "	1 5/8 "	5/8 " ....
10 "	1 3/4 "	5/8 " ....
11 "	1 1/2 "	1/2 " ....
11 "	1 1/2 "	5/8 " ....
11 "	1 5/8 "	1/2 " ....
11 "	1 5/8 "	5/8 " ....
11 "	1 3/4 "	1/2 " ....
11 "	1 3/4 "	5/8 " ....
12 "	1 5/8 "	1/2 " ....
12 "	1 5/8 "	5/8 " ....
12 "	1 3/4 "	1/2 " ....
12 "	1 3/4 "	5/8 " ....

Special Sizes made to Order.

Directions for Replacing Wringer Rolls.

Remove the washer or cog-wheel at the end of the shaft opposite the crank ; then take off the old roll and **clean the shaft thoroughly,** being careful to remove from it all rust or dirt. Place the plunger over the end of the shaft, and cover both completely with **Cement.** Be careful to cover every portion so that the roll will **slip easily.** Coat the inside of the roll also with cement; then place the shaft with the plunger over the end in a perpendicular position in a vise. When placing the hole of the roll to the end of the plunger, a sudden and powerful pull downward on the roll will bring it to its place. The hole of the roll should be at least ¼ inch less in diameter than the diameter of the shaft.

Price of Wringer Rolls   -   -   –   per lb., $0,75

RUBBER
COVERED ROLLERS.

SQUEEZE, PRESS, SIZE AND COUCH ROLLS.

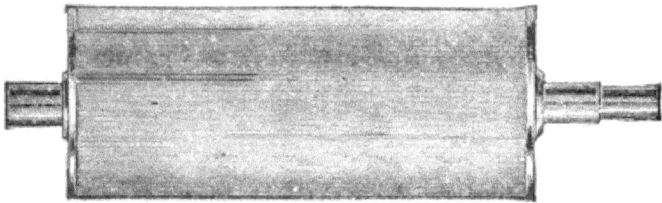

Guaranteed to give entire satisfaction.

In ordering, please state for what work the
Rolls are intended, and whether they
are to be run in hot or cold
liquid.

We prepare all our Rolls specially for the work
they are to do.

Price,   –   -   -   -   -   -   per lb., $1.00

Printers' and Lithographers' Blankets.

Used by Manufacturers of Printing and Lithograph Presses, also by Delaine, Calico and Paper Printers.

Width.	2-PLY. No. 16, 1-16 thick.	3-PLY. No. 14, 1-12 thick.	4 & 5-PLY. No. 11, 1-8 thick.
26 inches,	$5 00	$6 25	$7 25 per yard
30 "	5 50	6 75	8 25 "
32 "	5 75	7 00	8 75 "
34 "	6 25	7 50	9 75 "
36 "	6 50	7 75	10 25 "
38 "	7 25	8 50	11 25 "
40 "	7 50	8 75	11 75 "
42 "	8 00	9 50	12 50 "
44 "	8 50	10 00	13 50 "
46 "	9 50	11 00	14 50 "
48 "	10 50	12 00	16 00 "
50 "	12 00	14 00	18 00 "
52 "	14 00	16 00	20 00 "
54 "	16 00	18 00	22 00 "
56 "	18 00	20 00	24 00 "
58 "	20 00	22 00	26 00 "
60 "	22 90	24 00	28 00 "

FULL ROLLS contain 18 to 20 Yards, and are carried in stock.   SPECIAL LENGTHS cut or made to order.

Made Endless, or in any length desired, on special orders. The Printers' and Lithograhers' Blankets sold by us are acknowledged to be the very best in the market. We do not offer the cheaper grades.

PRICES ON APPLICATION.

ORGAN BELLOWS CLOTH.

			Sheeting.	Drill.
Dull Finished, 36 in. wide,	-	per yd.	$0.65	$0.85
" " 48 "	-	"	0.90	1.10

NURSERY SHEETING.

(Black or White.)

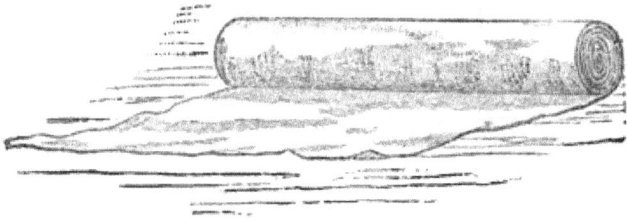

3/4 yard wide	-	-	-	per yard,	$0.70
4/4 " "	-	-	-	"	0.90
5/4 " "	-	-	-	"	1.20
6/4 " "	-	-	-	"	1.50
4/4 " " double coated	-		"		1.50

MACKINTOSHES.

FAC-SIMILE OF LABEL.

"MALTESE CROSS" BRAND

THE GUTTA PERCHA & RUBBER M'F'G. CO. OF TORONTO, L'TD

TRADE · MARK.

GUARANTEED NOT TO OPEN AT SEAMS

GUARANTEED NOT TO GROW HARD

ODORLESS MACKINTOSHES

Manufactured Solely by this Company.

☞See that your Mackintosh has a woven silk label in it as above, as this is the only brand which will successfully stand this climate.

Made from English and Scotch Tweeds.

WARRANTED NOT TO GROW HARD.

Odorless, Stylish, Durable, Tailor Fashioned, Sewn Seams.

See Next Page.

TWEED MACKINTOSHES.

WE take pride in the honor of being the first to successfully manufacture thoroughly reliable Mackintosh Garments in this country, and **we are to-day the only manufacturers in Canada of superior goods suitable for the finest trade.**

We guarantee our Mackintoshes to be thoroughly waterproof, and to remain soft and pliable in any climate. In addition to this, we offer them as superior in style, fit and finish to any similar goods on the market. By our process of proofing the cloths with Fine Para Rubber they are rendered **absolutely odorless,** and will so remain.

Experienced tailors superintend the manufacture of our Mackintoshes. The seams are sewn throughout. In the selection of attractive patterns, and attention to details of finish and comfort in a garment, we propose to be always abreast or ahead of the times.

SPECIAL ATTENTION

is called to our Custom Department, in which Mackintoshes for both **Gentlemen and Ladies** are promptly made to measure, thus securing to our patrons, results in fit, style and finish never before enjoyed by wearers of waterproof clothing.

☞**Ask your dealer for the "Maltese Cross" brand Mackintoshes, and see that they have the Maltese Cross labels in them,** (fac-simile on preceding page), **bearing our name and trade mark.**

Rubber Surfaced Clothing.

MEN'S AND BOYS'.

Officer's Coat.   Talma.

SIZES IN RUBBER COATS.

THE sizes in Men's Coats range from 36 to 46 inche
Chest measure, and are numbered for con
venience from 2 to 7, corresponding to the fo
lowing Chest Measurements :

2/36 in., 3/38 in., 4/40 in., 5/42 in.. 6/44 in., 7/46 in.

In Boys' Coats the range is from 20 to 34 inches
these are numbered 00, 0, 1, 2, 3, 4, 5 and 6, increasin
in Chest measurement 2 inches to each size as i
Men's Coats.

Sizes larger than the above, or variations from th
regular proportions, will be charged as "specials" a
slight additional cost.

A regular case contains 50 coats, assorted sizes.

SEE FOLLOWING PAGE.

Rubber Surfaced Clothing.
DULL FINISHED.

Fireman's Coat.

Sack Coats, on Sheeting, - - - -	$2.35
" " on Drill, - - - - - -	2.70
Officer's Coats, on Sheeting, - - -	2.60
" " on Drill, - - - - -	2.95
" " on Sheeting, printed back,	3.00
Boy's Sacks, on Sheeting, - - - - -	2.20
Boy's Officer's, on Sheeting, - - - -	2.40
Boy's Capes, on Sheeting, - - - - -	2.75
Men's Capes, on Sheeting, - - - -	2.85
" " on Drill, - - - - -	3.20
Reefing Jackets, on Sheeting, - - -	2.00
" " on Drill, - - - -	2.30
Mountaineer Coats, on Sheeting, 54 in. long,	3.15
" " on Drill, 54 in. long, -	3.50
Driver's Coats, double coated, fly front, - -	5.25
Firemen's Coats, double coated, fly front with Straps on Sleeves, and Snaps and Rings, or Automatic Buckles, - - - - - -	6.00
Talmas, on Sheeting, - - - - -	3.30
" on Drill, - - - - - - -	3.65

Sewn Seams 25 cents extra.

RUBBER CLOTHING.

(Continued).

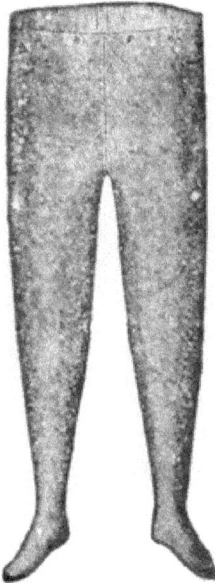

Fishing Pants.   Fishing Stockings.

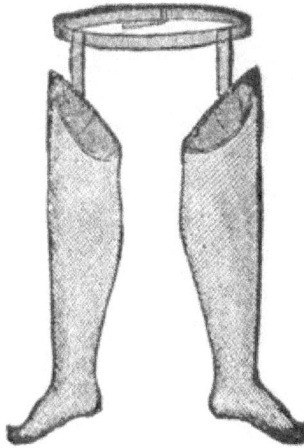

Pants, dull finished, per pair,   -   -   -   - $8.00

Stockings, dull finished, per pair,   -   -   -   6.00

LEGGINGS AND CAMP BAGS.

LEGGINGS.

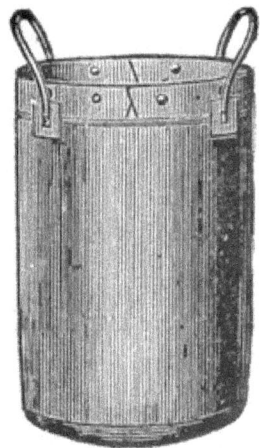

CAMP BAG.

LEGGINGS.

Men's Leggings, on Sheeting, per dozen, - $12.00

" " on Drill, per dozen - 14.00

Boy's " on Sheeting, per dozen, - 11.00

Subject to Discount.

CAMP AND NAVY BAGS.

Dull Finish, on Drill, each, - - - $4.00

" " on Duck, heavy, with Leather Trimmings, each, - - - 10.00

RUBBER APRONS.

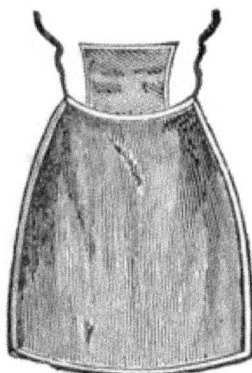

ICE APRON.   LADY'S APRON.

Ice Aprons, light   -   -   per doz. $27.00
"   "   medium,   -   -   "   30.00
"   "   heavy,   -   -   -   "   36.00
Ladies' Aprons, on Sheeting,   -   "   18.00

CAPE CAPS.

Lustre Finished, per doz.   -   -   - $6.00
Dull   "   "   -   -   -   7.00

WAGON APRONS.

Drill, with Pocket, Cemented, each,	-	$2.50
Drill, " Stitched, each,	-	-	2.20
Sheeting " Cemented, each,	-	2.25

CARRIAGE RUGS.

Tartan Lined, Cotton, each, - - $2.50

Fancy Lined, heavy, - - - - 3.50

Army and Poncho Blankets.

Camp and Army Blankets, 45 x 72, each, $2.00

" " " 45 x 66 " 1.80

Poncho Blankets, - - 45 x 72 " 2.50

Tarpaulins, Salvage Covers, Wagon Covers.

On Drill	-	per square yard	$1.25
" Duck	-	" "	1.75
" Drill, double coated,		" "	1.50
" Duck, " "	-	" "	2.00

Made any size, with grommets or eyelets in the border.

PIANO COVERS.

Drab Rubber Surface, Canton Lining.

54 x 96 inch, plain	each	$4.50
72 x 108 " "	"	5.00
Upright, small	"	9.00
" large	"	10.00

BILLIARD TABLE COVERS.

Drab or Black Rubber Surface.

6 x 12 feet	$7.00
7 x 12 feet	8.00
8 x 13 feet	10.00

Prices on Application.

....PRICE LIST....

OF

CARRIAGE CLOTHS

MANUFACTURED BY

THE GUTTA PERCHA & RUBBER MFG. CO.

OF TORONTO, Ltd.

Embossed Rubber Carriage Cloth.

		DRILL.	DUCK.
18 oz. 48 in. per yard		.69	.79
20 " " "		.71	.81
22 " " "		.73	.83
23 " " "		.75	.85
24 " " "		.77	.87
25 " " "		.79	.89
26 " " "		.81	.91
27 " " "		.83	.93
28 " " "		.85	.95
29 " " "		.87½	.97½
30 " " "		.90	1.00
31 " " "		.92½	1.02½
32 " " "		.95	1.05
33 " " "		.97½	1.07½
34 " " "		1.00	1.10
35 " " "		1.02	1.12
36 " " "		1.04	1.14
37 " " "		1.06	1.16
38 " " "		1.08	1.18
39 " " "		1.10	1.20
40 " " "		1.12	1.22

On Brown Drill or Duck, 5c. per yd. Net additional.
On Indigo Blue Drill, - 8c. " " "
On Green Drill, - - 10c. " " "

HORSE COVER, WITHOUT HOOD.

HORSE COVER, WITH HOOD.

See List Prices on next page.

HORSE COVERS AND HOODS.

	EACH
Lustre Sheeting, no Hoods, - - -	$4.00
" " with Hoods, - - -	6.00
Lustre Drill, no Hoods, - - - -	4.60
" " with Hoods, - - - -	7.00
Embossed Drill, no Hoods, - -	5.00
" " with Hoods, - - -	8.00
Loin Covers, on Drill, - - - -	3.00
" " on Drill, double coated, - -	4.50
" " on Duck, - - - -	4.00
" " on Duck, double coated, - -	5.50
Horse Hoods, separate, Lustre Sheeting, -	2.40
" " " Lustre Drill, - -	2.65

WAGON SPRINGS.

FLAT.   ROUND.

FLAT.

No. 1. 4 in. high, 2 in. thick,   -   per lb., 35c.
"   2. 3¾ "   "   1¾ "   "   -   -   "   "
"   3. 3½ "   "   1½ "   "   -   -   "   "
"   4. 3¼ "   "   1¼ "   "   -   "   "

Carried in stock.

ROUND.

Diameter, 2 in. to 6 in.; thickness, 1 in. to
3 inch   -   -   -   -   per lb., 60c.

Made to order only.

ANTI-RATTLERS.

Per gross pairs (in boxes)   -   -   - $5.00
In Strips, per lb.   -   -   -   -   -   .85

PROP BLOCK.

Prop Block, per foot, oval,   -   -   -   .35
"   "   "   round,   -   -   .35
"   "   Washers, per doz.   -   -   .55

Interfering Ankle Balls
ON LEATHER STRAPS.

Large Size, strapped   -   -   per doz. $3.70
Small   "   "   -   -   -   "   3.40
Ankle Balls, loose   -   -   per lb.   1.25

Elastic Interfering Bands.

Large Size,   -   -   -   -   per doz. $3.70
Small   "   -   -   -   -   "   3.40

PULLEY FILLING,

Or WIRE ROPE PACKING.

Price,   -   -   -   -   -   -   per lb. $1.00

GRAIN DRILL TUBES.

Special prices quoted on application for contract lots.

FRUIT JAR RINGS.

OF SUPERIOR QUALITY, EVEN THICKNESS, AND SIZES TO FIT PINT AND QUART JARS.

Quarts,   -   -   -   -   per gross $1.40
Pints,   -   -   -   -   -   ''   1.20

SPECIAL SIZES TO ORDER.

SPECIALTIES.

Bicycle Tires,
>Bicycle Inner Tubes,
>>Bicycle Treadles,
>>>Billiard Cushions,
>>>>Band Saw Bands,

Street Car Springs,
>Omnibus Springs,
>>Steam Drill Buffers,
>>>Locomotive Blocks,
>>>>Pump Buckets,

Gutta Percha, Crude Chips,
>Gutta Percha Sheet,
>>Gutta Percha Strips,
>>>Pure Para, Crude,
>>>>Pure Para, Refined,

Round Belts,
>Stuffing Box Rings,
>>Weather Strip Packing,
>>>Diaphragms, Moulded,
>>>>Unvulcanized Gum.

Special Prices on Application.

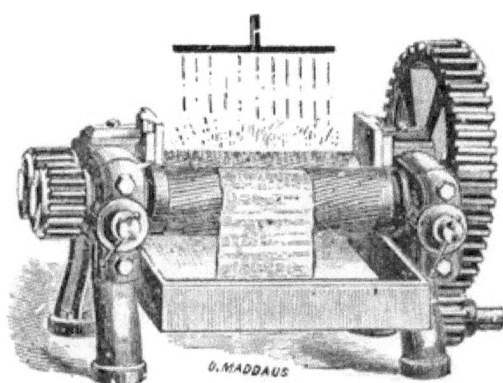

MILL FOR
WASHING CRUDE INDIA RUBBER.

MILL FOR BREAKING AND GRINDING
CRUDE INDIA RUBBER.

CALENDER

FOR

COATING COTTON
CLOTH AND DUCK

WITH

RUBBER.

Weight, - - - 60,000 Pounds.

Native Preparing Crude Rubber for Market.

INDEX.

MAMMOTH BELT ORDER.

MANF'd BY
The GUTTA PERCHA & RUBBER M'F'G. CO. of TORONTO LTD.
61 & 63 FRONT ST W.

for The CANADIAN PACIFIC RY
ELEVATOR AT
FORT WILLIAM ONT

LENGTH 295 FT
WIDTH 32 IN
2041 LBS

LENGTH 605 FT
WIDTH 36 IN
3540 LBS

LENGTH 85 FT
WIDTH 36 IN
519 LBS

LENGTH 825 FT
WIDTH 36 IN
4872 LBS.

LENGTH 35 FT
WIDTH 36 IN
217 LBS

LENGTH 260 FT
WIDTH 42 IN
1672 LBS

LENGTH 615 FT
WIDTH 36 IN
3681 LBS

LENGTH 589 FT
WIDTH 36 IN
3468 LBS

TOTAL WEIGHT 20,004 LBS.

www.ingramcontent.com/pod-product-compliance
Lightning Source LLC
Chambersburg PA
CBHW030541270326
41927CB00008B/1465